From Oxford, **Philip Mason** went to India where he served in the Civil Service for twenty years. Upon returning to England, he began a writing career that has since embraced some twenty-five books, including *The Men Who Ruled India* (under the pseudonym Philip Woodruff), *Kipling,* and *Christianity and Race.* Mr. Mason has traveled widely in Africa, the Caribbean, and Central and South America.

THE DOVE IN HARNESS

The Dove in Harness

PHILIP MASON

1817

HARPER & ROW, PUBLISHERS
New York, Hagerstown, San Francisco, London

FIRST U.S. EDITION

ISBN: 0-06-065468-6

LIBRARY OF CONGRESS CATALOG CARD NUMBER: 76-5143

76 77 78 79 80 81 10 9 8 7 6 5 4 3 2 1

Contents

FOR
HUGH NEWBOLD

Preface

This book is meant for the puzzled, not for the learned. It is for those who are sometimes aware of a purpose in the universe, of an eternity beyond the range of limited human minds, who are restless for a deeper understanding of their own occasional intimations, but who cannot reconcile their intermittent hopes and beliefs with what seems to them to be offered by orthodoxy. They shrink from anything so humdrum as a church service or a parochial committee. This short book does not attempt to find an answer for all the difficulties such people may feel. It does try to suggest one approach to Christianity as a practical way of life. It tries to show how a man can harness the dove of occasional inspiration to the bullock-cart of daily existence.

Some time ago I was invited to deliver in the winter of 1975 the sixteenth series of lectures sponsored by the Scott Holland Trustees. It was a daunting proposition. Henry Scott Holland, in whose memory the Trust was founded soon after his death in 1917, was for most of his life a Canon of St Paul's Cathedral; he refused various higher appointments because he believed that his special gifts as a speaker and writer were best employed there. The heart of his teaching is expressed in two ideas, which in his lifetime were often dissociated from each other, even by those who accepted each of them separately. He believed passionately that the centre of Christianity was the Incarnation and also that Christianity must find expression in a concern for the

social and economic life of contemporary man. These
beliefs the lectures – they take place every three years – have
in various ways expressed and illuminated. The series began
with R. H. Tawney, whose lectures developed into his
well-known book *Religion and the Rise of Capitalism* (1922).
Among his distinguished successors have been William
Temple, A. D. Lindsay and Michael Ramsey.

What place was there for me in such company as this? I
was neither theologian nor economist, neither sociologist
nor philosopher, nor in any professional sense historian.
But there was a problem which had been disturbing me for
fifty years. It had first worried me as an undergraduate. If
everyone did as the gospels commanded and took no
thought for the morrow, no corn would be sown or har-
vested, no ships would sail, no trains would run and we
should all starve together. It is with taking thought for
tomorrow that human society really begins; without that,
it is an animal association, a pack of wolves or baboons. If
Christianity seeks to destroy all the foresight and co-
operation that enable men to live together, how can
anyone take it seriously as a way of life?

Time to think things out – that is a need I have felt all my
life and constantly disregarded in favour of the trivial and
ephemeral. But, at seventy, every opportunity must be
seized; it is high time to make up one's mind and put on
record such evidence as one has gathered and such opinions
as one has formed. Further, a layman from his ignorance
may be able to speak to other laymen when a theologian is
hampered by the weight of his knowledge. So, in spite of
deep misgivings about lack of professional skills, I accepted
the invitation.

But when I started work on the lectures, the misgivings
were intensified. It was clear that a comprehensive treat-
ment was quite out of the question. I could not afford the
time to read all I should or the space to say all I wanted.
All I could attempt was to identify the problem as I saw
it, sketch the outlines of a discussion and suggest an ap-

proach. My aim must be to stimulate, not to satisfy, to start listeners on lines of thought they would work out for themselves.

The lectures were given in Oxford in the Michaelmas Term of 1975, that is, from October to December. I have always regarded the lecture as a mediaeval survival, tolerable before the invention of printing but a poor substitute for the printed page. With a book in his hand, the reader can raise his eyes and reflect on anything that requires consideration. But the listener has no power to switch the lecturer off so that he may pause for reflection, switching on when he is ready to give him his attention once again. This, however, is a disadvantage for the audience. For the speaker, if he means to write a book, there are compensations. Lectures may constitute a useful rehearsal. It is salutary to read one's words aloud; it sharpens self-criticism. Sometimes an audience will provide fresh insight. On the other hand, the style needed for a lecture is seldom quite right for a book, nor is it reasonable to expect ideas to fit themselves into six lectures of exactly equal length. My lectures had therefore to be reorganized and partly rewritten to make a book.

There was, however, a good reason for not rewriting entirely. In preparing the lectures, I had been conscious of making a journey. My own position had developed; I was far clearer in my own mind at the end than at the beginning. What I was examining was something I really felt as a problem—and still do, though I have made it less acute for myself. That sense of a journey would, I hoped, give the reader a feeling of movement and freshness which must not be allowed to disappear. It seemed best therefore to keep as close as I could to the original and not to exceed by much the original length.

For the same kind of reason, it seemed best to keep broadly to the plan adopted in the lectures of disclosing my own position step by step. No doubt it would be more logical to concentrate the attack—the arguments of my imaginary opponent – in the first part of the book, and to keep the more constructive approach for the second. But the effect would be depressing and this is, as I have said, a book for the puzzled, who will need some consolation by the way. So it seemed best in the book, too, to allow my own ideas to develop in stages, by means of interludes.

In a discussion of this kind, there are always two dangers. One arises from the use of metaphor. It is impossible to avoid metaphor; indeed, on such a subject it probably provides the only means of expressing ourselves. But however enlightening on one point, a metaphor is almost always misleading on another. It is as though one were engaged in marching round some gigantic Himalayan peak, thirty or forty miles distant, which can only be glimpsed every two or three days through the surrounding foothills and which every time presents a different face. It is like watching a great cloud illuminated by occasional rays of sunshine and changing its shape as it rolls on. So long as you keep changing your metaphors and remember how inadequate they must be, no harm will be done. But some metaphors become fixed and are taken literally; think of the absurdities that have been caused by attributing to an Eternal Purpose a position in space, equally primitive whether it is 'up there' or 'out there'. It is almost impossible to avoid using language which suggests that what is by definition Timeless is in time; it is hard to speak of a Cause or a Purpose without suggesting a method of operation that resembles the human. I can only plead that when I do this I am usually aware of it. But it would be very tiresome to the reader to make the point every time.

The other source of misunderstanding arises from unstated assumptions. It is easy for each party to a discussion to assume that the other accepts his own assumptions, or, on the other hand, that the other believes what he emphatically does not. But again it would be tedious to start the argument with a list of fundamental points of belief; I have tried to reveal mine gradually in the course of the main argument.

To write about religion, and particularly about what kind of conduct religion should encourage, carries a distasteful implication of smugness. But everyone has a religion, whether he knows it or not, and even if he explicitly rejects any formulated religion. Surely it is sensible to consider what one does believe and discuss it. And there is a good deal to be said for being clear about the meaning of beliefs that have influenced conduct for two thousand years and on which so much thought and argument have been spent. Have we got the Message yet? Our behaviour suggests that we have not. If we reject it, we should at least know what we are rejecting. My views have no more authority than anyone else's; the reader will probably not agree with me but I hope he will at least consider his reasons for disagreeing. One story has been constantly in my mind as I have written these pages; I have tried to feel more like the man who stood at the back of the church and asked for mercy than like the man who stood in front and thanked God he was not like other men.

P.M.

1976

I

The Lilies of the Field

I EMPTINESS AT THE HEART

In the rich part of the world today, there is emptiness at the heart. Surfeit of material goods has led to a hunger of the spirit. Motor cars and washing-machines make people no happier than their grandparents. Democracy is fly-blown; no one can any longer suppose that votes for everyone are an automatic voucher for justice, honesty or dignity. We have the knowledge and skill to feed the hungry but we cannot agree with each other long enough to make what we know effective. We are so frightened of each other that we spend on defence what would put an end to malnutrition and starvation. In anger at the injustice of the world, and in despair because they have nothing to believe in, the young turn to drugs, to freak philosophies, to cheap remedies.

Sometimes they turn to Eastern religions, though not always with much understanding or determination. But they do not – the young – very often or very noticeably turn to the traditional religion of Western Europe. Christianity is too respectable, they think; it is the religion of the very people who are responsible for the waste and corruption and misdirection at which they protest. Of course they are wrong about this; their elders, if they profess Christianity at all, disregard it in practice. They perceive obscurely that to take it seriously would undermine the self-interest – not to call it greed – which is the foundation of economic science and the cement that has so far held society together. They see in Christianity something which frightens and repels them; it is radical, it undermines their comfort, it demands sacrifice. And so they unobtrusively reject it, but what they fear in it is diametrically the opposite of what the young throw in its teeth – that it is too easy, that it has grown a middle-aged paunch and smells of hassocks in the pew.

It is the old who are right. The teaching of the gospels *is* subversive. Here then is my first big question. Does it make sense to profess a religion on which hardly anyone acts and which would destroy society if it were put into practice? Can Christianity, truly accepted, be a working creed? Can it present a practical framework for the conduct of life?

There is emptiness, I repeat, at the heart of Western society. Its unstated creed appears to be materialist; the pursuit of happiness – one of its stated aims – is taken to mean the pursuit of more pay and more holidays. But the materialist society does not seem to be working; when everyone adopts aims that are not only materialist but also narrowly selfish it begins to break down. It is certainly not making people happy. I am not sure, however, that there are many *convinced* materialists. Of course there are plenty of *practising* materialists, people who live as though material possessions were all they wanted, who pretend that death and eternity do not exist. Really convinced materialists are more rare, but it is not with them that I mean to argue. Indeed, argument with such people may be as pointless as trying to explain yellowness to a man blind from birth. On the other hand, there is a great deal to suggest that there are many, not only among the young, who would like to find in life something more than the material. It is with such people that I want to open a discussion.

They do not know where to turn. There are many obvious reasons for not turning to Christianity; for one thing, it demands time and effort. But the paradox I have just put as a question is perhaps another less obvious reason.

Christianity asks too much; it is so total, so absolute. Take it seriously and everything else collapses. It is not a point I have often heard discussed in sermons – yet to relate the actual words of the gospels to everyday life is surely essential if Christianity is to be taken seriously as a way of life. There are other implications too, big enough in themselves, but in my view secondary. Christianity is the foundation of the vast system that in Europe for fifteen hundred years has dominated philosophy, art, politics, architecture and law, and has spread from Europe over half the world. Christianity is the background of our whole culture, of all that we have arrogantly called civilization – and yet there is this contradiction at the heart of it. Do we really mean, angrily and impatiently, to reject our traditional religion and our traditional culture as well? Let us at least consider the paradox squarely before we make up our mind to so extreme a repudiation, and, to begin with, let us look briefly at the four main aspects of the difficulty – property, violence, sex and the self – and then come back to each of them in rather more detail.

2   THE PARADOX OF IMPRACTICABLE PERFECTION

Jesus of Nazareth was executed for subversive teaching. He said the poor were blessed, told men to turn the other cheek, told them to take no thought for the morrow. His followers for a time took him literally: they tried keeping all things in common, they experimented with a curious kind of sexless marriage, they kept out of politics. All this was because they expected the second coming and the end of the world. They thought they should anticipate heaven and live on earth almost as though they had already cast off the body.

But the end of the world did not come. They had to live in the world; they had to find ways of living *with* a world that was – on the whole and for most of the time and in varying degrees – hostile. Sometimes they were laughed at and disregarded; sometimes determined attempts were made to force them out of existence as a body of believers, and they had to choose between dying for their creed and giving it up. In general, for three hundred years, to be a Christian meant sacrifice. Then came the reversal. Christianity became the state religion of the Roman Empire. A persecuted and despised minority became the Establishment.

From that moment, the paradox became acute. Could the world be ruled in accordance with the teaching of an unpractical dreamer, a condemned revolutionary? High over Europe hung that tremendous symbol, the felon's gibbet, and nailed to it the tortured and emaciated figure of divine Man. Below it, the head of the Church sat on a golden throne; the peacock fans waved about his head. Abbeys and monasteries held broad lands and priceless treasures. The emperor's orb and sceptre were of gold; the knights of his noble orders stood around him – mailed, armed, with gilt spurs and gold-encrusted swords. In the name of the Prince of Peace, crusades were launched against the Saracens; in Provence the Albigenses were slaughtered. Nations professing to be Christian accepted as part of God's plan the injustices of the Ancien Régime in France, the Industrial Revolution in Britain, slavery in the United States, autocracy in Russia. That torn and wasted figure hung there silent.

A familiar story, you may say – the white-hot purity of the Master's radical zeal muddied and tarnished by the greed, the corruption, the readiness to compromise of his followers. But this is not quite the familiar story. The Church – by which for the moment I mean professing Christians in action – has lasted two thousand years and is still alive, demonstrating its life by the turmoil within it. The whole history, from its beginning to the present, is one of conflict – blinding revelations of light, simple men seeking the truth burned alive for their mistakes, wise men thoughtfully organizing and defining the truths they have been enabled to perceive; saints such as Francis of Assisi trembling on the brink of heresy and condemnation; periods of deadly apathy, periods of reforming zeal and outraged reaction, of bitter argument and obstinate strife, times of materialism and indifference; multiple division. Yet still, after so many centuries, there are martyrs ready to die for what they see as the Light.

So it is not quite the familiar story, simply because it goes on. Nor is it a matter of original teaching that was clear and simple being overlaid by the subtlety and compromise of followers. The paradox of impracticable perfection is there at the very heart of the Christian episode, from the beginning of its two-thousand-year course until today.

If you look at a history of the Church, you will find a great deal of discussion about matters on which men can only talk in metaphor—matters such as the nature of the Holy Trinity and the relation of the Holy Spirit to the Father and the Son—but very little, it seems to me, about the practical problems of how to live in the world in the light of the teaching of Jesus and of his life and death. Yet the difficulty was there from the start; you see it, for instance, in the story in the Acts of the Apostles about Ananias, who sold his property and handed in, to the common fund of the Christian community, what he said was the price he had received. It was not; he had held something back for himself. He was condemned, not for holding part back but for deceiving the community, but the story does show that to give everything was expected. What happened to that first experiment in communism? Why was it dropped?

The contradiction is there in all four gospels. In St John's Gospel, God loved the world; it was he who had made the world and he had seen that it was very good. But the Incarnate Word—who had been there in the beginning, without whom nothing was made that was made—had overcome the world; His disciples were not 'of the world' just as He Himself was not 'of the world'. Was the world then bad after all? In Matthew, Mark and Luke, the three synoptic gospels, men were told to take no thought what they should eat or drink, yet a society is taken for granted in which rich men let out their vineyards to husbandmen and employ stewards. It is wrong to build a tower carelessly on sand, but also wrong to build a barn to house your surplus crops. Take no thought for the morrow—but, when the foolish bridesmaids do just that, they are locked out of the Wedding. It is wrong to lay up treasure on earth —but he was a wicked servant who did not put his one pound in the bank.

Does it make sense then, in terms of practical life, to want to be a Christian—for there is a sense in which it is presumptuous to say one *is* a Christian? Not, I think, unless you face squarely the contradictions at the heart and the paradoxes in which you will be involved. Let me state some of the difficulties which seem to me to arise about property, about the use of force, about the self in politics and art, about sex and the family, about the continual need for compromise if one is to get anything done. At this stage, I am the Devil's advocate, putting a criticism that I think is felt more often than it is expressed.

Take property first. Jesus told the rich young man to give all he had to the poor. But if everyone did that, the world would starve; there would be no one to fill the begging-bowls. If no one had any thought for the morrow, chaos would be upon us. A man cannot wring a living from the soil unless he has at least a pair of bullocks and a plough. He must save some seed for next year. Where do you draw the line? Those who profess to be Christians and take part as members in Western society are open to a double attack. They ignore Christian principles; they do not live like the lilies of the field; they are rich and self-indulgent; they spare very little for the beggar who lies at their door. But if on the other hand they did follow the teaching of the gospels, give away all that they possessed and take no thought for the morrow, the trains would not run nor ships arrive; we should all go hungry. What sort of religion is it that would bring disaster if everyone followed its teaching?

There is a similar contradiction over the use of force, though in a sense it is the other way round. If *everyone* turned the other cheek when struck and if the assailant — overcome by remorse — always and immediately repented, all would be well. But of course it is not like that. The need to turn the other cheek does not arise unless there is an aggressive assailant, and he does not always repent. If Christians alone did turn the other cheek and forgive unto seventy times seven, they would be at the mercy of the megalomaniac dictator, the hijacker and the assassin. And in practice, nations supposed to be Christian have engaged in the most frightful violence. The young idealist may well complain that Christians do not live up to their ideals; the shrewd materialist may retort that it is just as well they do not. Both alike may ask how anyone can profess to be a Christian.

Indeed, both critics may go further. Biological progress has been the result of aggression; plants as well as animals live at the expense of their neighbours. The species improves because the weakling goes to the wall and is trodden under foot; cherish the weak and the species will rot. Can the God of Nature really mean man to follow quite another rule? In politics and business, success demands an element of ruthless self-advertisement that is quite out of keeping with the Sermon on the Mount. How can you improve the world unless you first fight your way to the top and get some influence? Yet the great Christian teachers have said: 'Meek thyself! Naught thyself! Overcome thyself!'

Art too, demands ruthlessness; ruthless discipline of the self, certainly and always, but also sometimes the ruthless exclusion of friends and family. It is hard for an artist not to be an egotist and he will not finish his book or his picture unless he regards it as, for the moment at any rate, all-important. He must come near to idolatry while he is immersed. Nor is it, except perhaps in the very greatest, a selfless idolatry; it is often near to self-worship. And again, art presupposes both toiling peasant and munificent patron – a complex society in which some people build the houses and grow the corn, while others have leisure to appreciate the artist's work and a surplus with which to pay him. Art is inextricably entwined with money as well as aggression. How much harder to sell is a book written in a truly Christian spirit than one sharp with malice! So might the shrewd materialist argue. 'Thou hast conquered, O pale Galilean, and the world has grown grey with thy breath!' That was how it seemed to the young Swinburne and, although today it can hardly be said that the Galilean has conquered, many might argue that the world would grow grey if he did. Is art, then, too, at odds with Christianity? Is the Puritan right?

Both sex and the family raise the same kind of question. The marriage of one man and one woman and the family – in the sense of father, mother and children – have long been regarded in the West as a Christian institution. But the earliest Christians were doubtful about marriage. There would be none in heaven and they were not sure it was needed on earth. At best, it was a grudging concession to human weakness. Today many Africans regard the family of two generations as cold and individualist, because it neglects grandparents and cousins, while to some young people in the West it seems stuffy and claustrophobic. They find it repugnant to be tied by any bond but their own will at a given moment. They share with many Africans a feeling that Christianity has been negative about sex. On the one hand, say the young, their elders, who say they are Christians, have not lived up to their ideals; they have connived at prostitution, they have been furtive, hypocritical, and obsessed with sex; on the other, they have denied the spiritual beauty of something good and joyous. Once again, Christians have failed to live up to their principles and once again the principles must be wrong because they are out of keeping with nature.

At every turn, professing Christians are up against some form of the same dilemma. We proclaim the Word made Flesh, the Light that came into the world – and, in that Light, the thought of compromise is horrible. We want to reject any obedience less than perfect. Yet in practice, human society is based on compromise. Politics is always a compromise between different interests. It is the fanatic who will not compromise who wrecks the work of peace-makers; it is his intemperate obstinacy that leads to strikes, assassinations, wars, persecutions. Ever since the first Pentecost, there have been men trying to work out a way of following the Light in the world – that is to say, trying to find a working compromise between a literal obedience that would bring world disaster and a disregard that would mean spiritual death. Indeed, that is almost a definition of the Church; conflict and compromise are its essence. Far from being infallible, the Church *needs* continual conflict and criticism, the stimulus of dangerous visionaries, radical saints like Francis, heretics like Savonarola, recurring re-minders that it is becoming greedy and worldly and hard of heart. Yet without foresight and planning and careful husbanding of assets there is chaos. How can men harness the dove of inspiration to the bullock-cart of everyday life?

Let us begin by looking in more detail at one aspect of the paradox, that which concerns property.

2

The Rich Young Man

I RADICAL TEACHING

It was because his teaching was subversive that Jesus was put to death. I would go further; I think he was killed because of the social and economic implications of the teaching, though I would not make too much of that point. The Jews were a people who thought in terms of a religious state, and for them the charge of blasphemy was the surest way of rousing hostility. To their own people, that was the charge the rulers made; to the Romans, they charged him with political subversion, but that was clearly false; he had been careful to avoid the easy line of stirring up nationalist feeling. They ignored other similar movements, referred to by Gamaliel in Acts, which died away by themselves. Why was it so important to have Jesus killed, and by means as degrading and humiliating as possible? Because, surely, the ruling class felt threatened, not only by direct personal attacks, but by teaching that would have upset the whole basis of the society that gave them wealth and privilege and power. 'If people cease to respect their betters, they will cease to respect the Temple; we shall have no hold on them', they must have said. 'Where will it end?' They were aware of a feeling of disturbance, of distaste, of fear, and this they would formulate as blasphemy, probably without being aware of the other implications; 'social' and 'economic' were not words they knew. But what they felt was much what the rulers of England felt at the time of Peterloo, when it seemed that the dangerous teaching of the French Revolution might spread to England and that here, as in France, the rich might swing from lamp-posts or mount the scaffold.

However that may be, there can be no doubt of the impression which the teaching of Matthew, Mark and Luke is likely to have on a direct and simple mind reading those gospels for the first time and thinking about property. It is radical and ultimately subversive. The message is for the poor; the rich, the teachers, the lawyers, the rulers, are 'they'. Property is at best a hindrance to the kingdom of God, that is, to a spiritual life; sometimes it is so dangerous that it must be got rid of. In Luke especially, there is sometimes a note of triumphant hostility to the rich and their heartlessness; it is sounded in the Magnificat, where the rich are sent empty away, the humble and meek exalted; it is heard in the parable of Dives and Lazarus – which is not in Matthew or Mark – and it is particularly significant in Luke's version of the Beatitudes. Everyone knows the more comfortable form in which the Beatitudes occur in Matthew: 'Blessed are the poor in spirit...' But in Luke it is: 'Blessed are you poor...' – without qualification. 'Blessed are you that hunger *now*...' And the contrast follows at once: 'Woe unto you that are rich... Woe unto you that are full...' There are of course parables that take wealth and social difference for granted, but they are usually making a point about something else. The story of the foolish bridesmaids, for instance, is about being ready for a spiritual revelation and so are the several sayings about servants not ready for their master's coming.

Here there is a point to be made about style, which leads on to one about teaching. Hebrew – I am told, for I have no knowledge of it – is weak in abstract nouns and in adverbs; this makes for a direct style, for the use of images and metaphors. You do not say: 'punish severely' but: 'chastise with scorpions'. You do not say: 'He shall take great care of his people' but: 'He shall feed his flock like a shepherd'. Aramaic followed the habits of Hebrew. And the gospels, written down in Greek, record teaching spoken in Aramaic

and addressed to an audience of simple people, never far
from fields and sheep, people leading a life very like that of
the villagers to whom I used to talk in Northern India.
With such people, you learn to make one point at a time, if
possible by a concrete illustration, by poetic analogy, if you
can, rather than by reasoned exposition. They understand
by intuition rather than by reason. 'What milk are you getting here?' I heard a junior Indian official say to a villager
who was hanging about like a half-weaned calf near the
map we were making of the village fields. He ought to have
been a hundred yards away, at the far end of the measuring
chain, pointing out the boundaries of his own cultivation.
He understood at once. It is just because the teaching is
expressed intuitively, in stories, in the language of poetry,
in this simple peasant style, that it has lived in people's
minds. And it is because they usually make one point at a
time that the parables sometimes contradict each other
directly, as proverbs do.

Here I must say something about my view of the gospels
as evidence. When Henry Scott Holland was writing and
teaching,[1] he took trouble to answer what was then a
fashionable criticism of Christianity, that Paul had corrupted
the simple teaching of Jesus as set out in the gospels. Scott
Holland emphasized the fact that most of Paul's letters are
earlier than the gospels; the church for whom Paul wrote
was already in being when his followers decided to collect
the sayings and doings of Jesus. They wanted to record
them while there were still men who remembered them.
The gospels were first read to a community of believing
persons, with traditions of what the teaching had been,
already familiar with many of Paul's ideas and with an
established practice, a liturgy, a way of life and a system of
belief. There was already an orthodoxy, of which what
Paul was saying and what Jesus had said were both parts —
one expressed in terms of intuition and the other more in
terms of intellect. What the believers now heard they
compared with what they remembered. They were people

much less dependent on the written word than most of us are today and therefore with better memories. Without the memories of the illiterate, we should not have the gospels. We should not have Homer either.

But this argument, still I think valid, is today faced by a scepticism much more extreme. There are modern writers who, starting from just the point Scott Holland made, contend that it is impossible to disentangle either the personality or the teaching of the historical Jesus. The gospels, they say rightly, were written for a purpose, to proclaim a truth. They are therefore propaganda and historically unreliable and since there are some discrepancies, no reliance – they seem to argue – is to be placed in them at all. But this is a *non sequitur*. Because there is a mistake in one detail of a narrative, it does not follow in logic that the whole story is fictitious. And it is contrary to what is generally known of human behaviour to suppose that any narrative will be entirely and exactly accurate. It misunderstands the nature of evidence as it occurs in practice.

Of course the gospels were written with a purpose. What communication is not? Even an academic thesis is meant to persuade someone of something, if it is no more than the competence of the writer. But not all communications are false. And the ends of truth and justice are defeated if it is supposed that one discrepancy destroys the validity of everything else a witness has to say. I am again reminded of my Indian experience, when at one time I spent most of my working day listening to evidence. Much of it was fabrication. Indian peasants regarded the British law courts as an alien device and litigation as a trial of skill. They expected a magistrate to believe at most half of what they said and so – like a carpet-seller putting up his price because he expects you to beat him down – they added a good deal to the original facts. But to dismiss a case because both the parties had exaggerated was not to do justice. There was a truth somewhere behind the evidence. Often there remained, when you had discounted the embroidery, some undeniable residual fact—injuries recorded by a doctor, a house burned down, perhaps a corpse. What was the explanation of *that*? You had to consider the probabilities and the contradictions, the unwilling admissions, the material evidence, and get as near the truth as you could. Only a pedant—a man steeped in law books who really did not understand how things happened in a village—would insist that because part of the evidence was suspect, none of it could be believed. Such a man took a cheap easy way to avoid the decision it was his business to make.

Or come nearer home today. Two cars have been in collision. The more violent the accident has been, the less likely it is that you will get agreement from passengers or spectators as to the speed at which the cars were travelling and as to the exact circumstances. But that does not mean it did not happen. There on the road is the shattered glass; there lies the twisted frame of the car. There, perhaps, is blood and a broken body.

I am not suggesting that the evidence in the gospels is of the same order as that I used to hear in India—though some recent writers seem to think so. There is a great deal of agreement between the accounts and when they were written down there were people still living who remembered what had happened. But there *are* discrepancies. For example, Matthew's story of the flight to Egypt can hardly be reconciled with Luke's of the presentation in the temple. In Matthew, Herod's police are looking for the child to kill him—and the Holy Family fly to Egypt. In the other, the family go quite openly to the temple in Jerusalem to make an offering in accordance with traditional Jewish custom, forty days after the birth of a male child. Since Luke seems to have consulted the mother of Jesus, or perhaps had access to a source who was close to her, while Matthew is trying to show that a prophecy has been fulfilled, Luke is to be preferred.[2]

Nonetheless, when all the discrepancies have been taken into account, there are certain residual facts which seem to me undeniable. This man did live and teach and die; his teaching carries with it the stamp of a definite personality; there is a style and ring to his recorded sayings that convinces. We are often near to the actual words he used. The public discourses may sometimes have been prepared beforehand and he may have repeated them more than once; it seems likely that they were repeated by his followers to each other, and told again to fresh audiences. That is one fact. Another is that in spite of persecution his followers continued to believe he was in some special sense still alive after death; they repeated his sayings, based their whole lives on their beliefs about him and were ready to die for them. It is another fact that this life and death and teaching changed history – bisected time, as T. S. Eliot says.[3] Jesus knew that he was the promised one for whom the Jews had hoped and he said so; he perceived that the coming of the promised one was not to be, as they had supposed, in clouds of fire and glory but in human form, in poverty and pain. And that changed the world. I leave out of account for the moment the sense of personal guidance and companionship which millions of people have felt. I am putting the case coldly – at its lowest. It is not my purpose at present to discuss the full meaning of those residual facts; what I am saying is that they cannot be brushed aside; they are the central data of my problem, which is whether the teaching of Christianity provides a practical framework for the conduct of life. And I am led to the broad preliminary conclusion that what we have does represent the teaching of Jesus.

2 A UNIVERSAL FORMULA

Let me turn back to the rich young man. It was the answer to him which set me thinking about this difficulty fifty years ago. I read Kant's principle of conduct, that a man should act in such a way that he could regard his action as in accordance with a law proper for all other men. Kant was trying to find a formula, a test that a man could apply to his own behaviour: 'Would I think this particular act of mine right if somebody else were to do it?'[4] That is a reasonable test so far as it goes – but it is going too far to say that the act must be right for everyone. It works with the simplest kind of moral decision. Imagine, for instance, that I see how, without being detected, I can kill someone who has information I want to suppress. I cannot suppose this would be right for everyone so I must not do it. That, however, is not very helpful; I know the answer already, unless I am a pathological paranoiac. And you have only to apply the formula to a more difficult case to see how unhelpful it is.

Suppose you are a trustee of public funds and you consider that the principal servant of the trust is running it on lines not in accordance with its purpose. You do not doubt his integrity or good faith. To look at the problem of what you should do from the point of view of Kant's universal principle is only the first step. You know that you have no personal malice; on the contrary, you may have a personal liking. You know you do not want to do him personal harm. But you know also that personal feelings must not be allowed to stand in the way of your duty as a trustee. You have to consider the purposes of the trust and how far circumstances have changed – whether changed circumstances really demand a new policy – what damage you think is being done to the real purpose of the trust. All this you have to weigh against the personal considerations. A point may be reached where you must either acquiesce in misuse of funds or do that man harm. It is all a matter of weighing, of more or less, not of any absolute formula.

Or again let us suppose that your son, who is at the right age, wants to spend five years of his life learning to play the violin. To reach the standard he wants, he must abandon, at least for those five years, specialized training for any other technical career, such as medicine or engineering. The decision obviously depends on your son's musical ability, his aptitude for the instrument, and the opportunities there might be, if he was not good enough, for training in whatever would be his second choice as a career. To put the question into general terms is impossible without making it either answer itself or leave out a great deal that is important. Is it best for a person to do what he is best at doing? No one would hesitate over that, stated as a general proposition, any more than over the question of the murder. But it leaves out the vital question or what the boy *is* best at, how his best compares with the general average and whether he might not lead a fuller life if he decided, let us say, to make medicine his profession and give his spare time to an orchestra.

It seems to me now that Kant was misguided in trying to look for a universal formula as to what one should actually do. The wider its application, the less its practical value. Anything at all difficult to decide involves comparisons; it is a matter of better and worse, not good or bad, and in the end is a special case and intensely personal. A universal law as to the *spirit* in which one should act is quite another matter; no one can turn 'love God and love thy neighbour' into a proposition that merely answers itself.

3   THE FRANCISCAN EXPERIMENT

All the same, I *was* impressed fifty years ago with Kant's universal principle. On the other hand, I was fired by the simplicity and whole-heartedness of Francis of Assisi, by his joyous devotion to his calling as the troubadour of God. He read the gospels and heard the answer to the rich young man: 'If you would be perfect, go, sell what you possess and give to the poor.' He listened to the instructions with which the apostles were sent out: 'Take no gold nor silver nor copper in your belts, no bag for your journey nor two tunics, nor sandals nor a staff.' And he did exactly that. But I saw that if everyone did as Francis did, all would starve together. The Papal authorities saw it too. There was hesitation at Rome as to whether permission should be given for the first steps towards making a properly constituted Order of that first little band of devoted servants of the Lady Poverty. Partly, this was because there was some fear that they might be tainted with the Albigensian heresy and in particular the doctrine that matter was evil. But, even without the Albigensians, there was good reason to hesitate. Francis had twelve followers. The Papal Court must have foreseen how much more difficult it would be to stick to the life of holy Poverty when his followers were numbered in hundreds and in thousands. It is told how once a whole town wanted to follow Francis, old and young, men and women, married and single, and he had to reverse the current of his preaching and beg them to take care and consider carefully, to think what they were doing. It was perhaps with a tender scepticism that after long delay the Papal Court agreed to what Francis asked.

The long history of his order – with its many fissures and schisms, its great glories and martyrdoms – spirals, like a bean round a pole, on the one theme of struggle with the impracticable perfectionism of its founder. It began when he was still alive; he had to interrupt his mission to Egypt and hurry back to Italy because his Vicars were compromising the fidelity he had vowed to Poverty. There must be no property at all, he had said, and he had been disturbed when one of the brothers had referred to the hut of leaves and branches in which he had spent the last few nights as: 'Your cell'. It was not *his* cell; he had nothing. He must sleep somewhere else that night.

And yet some compromise was inevitable. Even he had had to compromise when Clare had listened to his preaching and determined that she too would follow Poverty. No one thought that women could live as the brothers did; it would have been a scandal. He must beg that Clare and her sisters should be received as guests in Benedictine houses – and thus they would have a share in Benedictine wealth.

He was disturbed when one of his brothers first entered a university. A scholar would have to possess books – and there was only one book anyone needed.

In 1227, within a year of Francis's death, the election of the first minister-general turned on a manifest violation of Francis's ideal. Elias of Cortona, who had been Francis's Vicar, was the obvious choice, but it was he who had begun building the great basilica and monastery at Assisi. It was his settled policy to organize the brothers, to make the loose fraternity Francis had founded into an Order. Elias was rejected and another chosen – ineffective but faithful to Poverty. The pendulum swung back. Three years later Elias was restored to the leadership and elected minister-general. Some of Francis's first companions were persecuted because they wanted to keep his instructions literally; Brother Leo and others of his dearest friends were scourged and Brother Bernard, the first disciple, 'spent a year hiding in the forests and mountains, hunted like a wild beast'.

Again there was a swing and Elias was deposed in 1239; by now, there were three parties clearly recognized within the order – the Zealots, who stuck exactly to Francis's spirit, the Moderates, and, at the other extreme, the Compromisers who had really abandoned the cult of Poverty. Controversy continued; victory swung to and fro between the Zealots and the Moderates. Should a 'moderate use' of this world's goods be allowed or 'a poor and scanty use?' Less than a hundred years after Francis's death, four of the Zealots were publicly burned at the stake at Marseille as obstinate heretics. Later still, the Order split into three distinct organizations, the Conventuals – who lived in monasteries and were allowed to own property jointly though not individually like other orders – the Observants and the Capuchins, both of whom tried to follow Francis more closely. Their major disputes, their reforming movements, all turned on the ideal of absolute poverty and how far it had to be modified.

All this controversy was about making life possible for those who had actually decided to follow Francis. The danger that the whole population might embrace poverty does not seem to have risen again. Indeed, perhaps here we have the simple common-sense answer to the question that began to worry me fifty years ago—it has never been very likely that everyone would take the advice given to the rich young man.

4 A MISGUIDED SEARCH

The usual answer to my question is that this was not advice for everyone. The rich young man had a special vocation to poverty. And there is a great deal in this. But it has always left me a little unhappy. Are there, then, *two* classes, the called and the not called? Are there—as the Gnostics taught—Perfecti or Illuminati, Chosen Spirits, predestined to a higher state of Being? I have never been able to understand how a humane mind could accept a doctrine of predestination in the strictest sense—that some are chosen before birth to be good and some to be bad and that there is no escape. It seems utterly opposed to the characteristic ethical note of the gospels—what really distinguishes their teaching about conduct from the best of Greek philosophy and the best of the Old Testament. I mean the tale of the Prodigal Son and that battery of metaphors and analogies that go with it—the lost sheep, the lost coin, the joy over the sinner that repents—and the cult of Mary Magdalene. It is personal choice that counts and what the Brahmans, the priests, the elders of the kirk, count as reckless and vicious living is all drowned in generous forgiveness if the penitent's choice is made in love and tears. Again—if the call is not for everyone—how am I to know whether it is 'for me'? Add to this, too, one more uneasy uncertainty. Why will the *poor* be really better off if they are presented with this dangerous commodity, money, which it seems I am so much the better for getting rid of? The Devil's argument, indeed, you may say to that, but there is a logic to it in contrast to the spirit of paradox.

The unease remains. Poverty is a vocation, perhaps a sacrament, for a chosen few. I understand – with the intellect. But we who live in Britain and America are all of us rich in the sense used in the gospels. We wear fine linen and fare sumptuously compared with the millions of India. We know where the next meal is coming from. I do not feel any happier if I am told that it is the spirit in which we enjoy these things that is important. It opens the way to an easy complacency and a personal hypocrisy; it leads to all that we dislike in what was once the soup-kitchen attitude.

As I look back, it now seems clear that fifty years ago I was involved in that misguided search for a clear simple answer – yes or no – that has caused so much trouble in human affairs. How comfortable it would be! 'Back in the army again, Sergeant', with nothing to do but what you're told – the one clear aim to win the War! How many systems have been built up that have taken away all that agonizing need for decision, that have buried individual freedom in minute rules about cleaning the outside of the cup and giving away exactly a tenth of all you possess – down to a tenth of the parsley and chives you grow in your garden! A rule for every contingency – a pigeon-hole for every human type – how easy it would make things! And of course his challenge to all this was a big part of what made Jesus so threatening to the rulers of the Church. They had it all so beautifully arranged! You didn't talk to Samaritans or tax-collectors – black men, foreigners, skinheads, fascists, communists. You knew just what you could do on the Sabbath and what you could not; you kept the rules about food and washing and fasting and giving alms – and now this tiresome man comes and upsets it all by devastating questions about doing good on the wrong day! What is worse, he actually does it – and puts us in the dilemma of either approving of what we know to be wrong or appearing to disapprove of an act of mercy and healing.

It was against the same tightly woven fabric of exact

compliance with minute regulation that Paul wrestled
with all the force of a fiery intellect just converted. Behind
all his tangled – and often clearly circular – argument lies
his own sudden blinding moment of vision. Now that he
had seen the Light, he knew that the Law killed but the
Spirit gave life. A man must decide each case as it came
to him; he could not fall back on a system of hard and fast
rules. And this is implicit in Jesus' own method of teaching,
by parables, one point at a time. For that young man, it was
right to give up property; it is always wrong to make an idol
of property; it may be right to look on it as a trust to be
used for the service of a master. It is wrong to be envious
about it and to worry about what other people get – that is to
say, about what are now called 'differentials'. Take no thought
for the morrow – don't be always fussing about a future you
can't possibly foresee – but, on the other hand, if you are
building a house, do see that it has proper foundations.

It is teaching that lays enormous emphasis on the value
of each individual and on each individual decision. But it is
far indeed from being 'individualism'. Indeed, Charles
Williams, one of the most deeply – if rather eccentrically –
Christian of this century's English writers, regards 'co-
inherence' as the essence of Christianity, and by that he
means being parts of a whole, physical *and* spiritual, members one of another. It is taken for granted, in the gospel
world, that people will go to work and be paid for their
work; the institutions with which everyone is familiar are
not attacked – not even slavery. Indeed, a slave is told to
go back to his master. Paul argues that, though he had worked with his hands to keep himself, he might justifiably have
asked the faithful to support him. The attempt to make an
exact rule – to have all things in common – cannot have
lasted more than a few years.

Jesus took for granted the existence of a social structure;
he attacked, sometimes fiercely, the spirit in which it
operated. What happened after his life and death – his
followers came to perceive – was that a new spiritual

structure had been superimposed on the old. There was a City of God as well as a City on earth; man was a citizen of both and, in a sense, to define the new relationship between his two sets of obligations was the main task of the Church – of the struggling, seeking, mass of Christ's people – for the next two thousand years. It is central to what this book is about.

There is another closely linked question, which throws light on this. Paul – tied though he was within a binding system of mental training – had the kind of live mind that is always struggling with difficulties to which he never finds answers that satisfy him altogether. He was concerned about differences within the Christian community. There had to be differences, because people had different gifts; there were bound to be inequalities. But the differences, he insists, are differences within a whole and the relationship between the parts is, as we should say today, organic; it is like the parts of the body, in which hands and feet may serve the brain but all alike feel an injury to one. There is no simple, hard and fast, mechanical relationship.

That metaphor of the body and its parts has interested political philosophers from Plato to Hobbes. It lies also at the mythological foundation of Hinduism, in which priests, warriors and cultivators took their origin from different parts of the Creator's body. It is illuminating about kingdoms in the earthly dimension; it suggests, for example, that a king who does not feel the pain of his people is no true king. But this is not enough to provide a basis for the whole of human conduct. It needs the new dimension that arises when the City of God is superimposed on the earthly kingdom. This alone makes sense of man's life. To be a good citizen of the earthly kingdom alone will not meet the hunger at man's heart. It is easy to picture a man who has paid all his taxes, lived in peace with his neighbour and filled in every form correctly – but who is starved by loneliness and by the lack of joy and compassion at the very centre of his being.

The paradox of impracticable perfection shows itself in four main areas. A brief look at property, the first of the four, suggests that they cannot finally be separated. Let us therefore postpone conclusions about this till we have looked at the other three. The kind of approach we are looking for will apply to them all. But before going on to the others, there are certain rules for the discussion, certain ways of setting out the pieces on the board, which need explaining because they affect the way I approach the subject. So let us put some of these in an interlude before resuming the main argument.

3

First Interlude

I LARKS AND CRAB-APPLES

First of all, in the field of human behaviour which concerns us most deeply, in relation to our most profound beliefs, I am impervious to the kind of argument which assumes that there is only one explanation for a certain kind of behaviour, an explanation which rules out all others. I do not believe that there is only one kind of truth. I am deaf to the man who begins: 'Now a statement is either true or not true ... ' His kind of argument may sometimes apply in the field of mathematics or of physical science, though even there I believe that a physicist and a chemist will give you quite different accounts of a given object.[1] And I am told that there is a kind of geometry on a curved surface in which the three angles of a triangle do not make two right angles. There is always a relation between the observer and the object observed; no two observers are alike and no observer is omniscient. The ancient story of the five blind men who came back with such conflicting reports on the elephant is still true – poetically true, psychologically true, imaginatively true.

But the moment you get into the field of behaviour, the dimensions of truth seem to be immensely more varied. For centuries, poets have thought that when a lark twinkles up from the downland grass into the sky and pours out a tiny waterfall of song, it is expressing its joy in existence – and some would have said proclaiming the glory of God. Today ornithologists tell us the male is warning rivals off its territory. Surely all these statements are true, but in different dimensions. Three added to two makes five – but in certain circumstances three added to two makes an unlawful assembly. And three added to two may sometimes make a happy family. The abstract proposition needs living detail to turn it into something warm and real and alive. You cannot read poetry as though it were algebra; the symbols do not always have the same value. And in the deepest regions of the human spirit we are much nearer poetry than algebra.

It seems to me to follow from this principle that one should expect the belief of individuals to have different dimensions at different times. I do not merely mean that we have moods. Nor do I mean only that we believe at different levels of intensity at different times. That certainly, but I suggest also that belief should sometimes be framed with a closely reasoned intellectual component, shot with scepticism about human formulations, and at other times with a simple and quite literal acceptance of the truth behind the formulation, an acceptance which for the moment involves taking the formulation itself quite uncritically. This is, I think, what Russian Orthodox writers mean by 'taking the head down into the heart'. It is an *act* of belief, a conscious decision, and probably for many of us a decision taken once for all and yet renewed every day.

That is one principle which runs through all the arguments in this book. The other is a way of looking at freedom and the meaning of freedom in relation to man's destiny. I came to it myself simply from trying to grow things in the garden. I cannot be happy with any system of belief that does not account for the difference between a Cox's Orange Pippin and a crab-apple from the hedge. Man has improved the apple, the rose, the grain of wheat far beyond what was achieved by the processes of evolution. In other words, there is something left unfinished in the material world, as well as in the nature of man, which can only be finished with man's help. It was left to man to develop strains of rust-free wheat – and with every improve-

ment there went always the possibility of dangerous side-
effects. And it seems to follow from this that we should
expect to find in the gospel a revelation of Light and Power
that was simple but not fully explicit. It was left to man
to work the consequences. A Light came into the world,
and it was for man to understand it—or to fail. It was
an offer of partnership, of sonship, the chance of taking part
in the joyful work of creation. Here as everywhere else, in
every advance, there is the possibility of a deeper corruption if we go wrong. I do not therefore look at the gospels
by themselves, in isolation; I do not expect the gospels to
tell me, in a blinding flash, all that has been worked out in
two thousand years. I expect to find there outlines, a framework, suggestions, signposts and clues. 'Christianity' means
not only that vision of Light but all that has happened since
—all the follies and cruelties and revelations and achievements of two thousand years. Inspiration was not cut off,
as you turn off a tap, in A.D.33. It went on; it still goes on.
We have a Church in being, still building a tradition, still
adapting and interpreting what that Light revealed. And
that is because we have this supreme, incredible, dangerous
gift of freedom. I came on the point suddenly the other day,
put in a nutshell, in the most unexpected place: 'God is
the freedom who allows freedom to others.'[2] But was it
right to give us freedom?

2   THE GRAND INQUISITOR

'Was it right to give us freedom?'

Let us put that question again in a more dramatic form.
Let me remind you of Dostoevsky's Grand Inquisitor, in
The Brothers Karamazov. The story is a parable of man's
freedom. It comes within the framework of a conversation
between two of the three brothers, Ivan and Alyosha. Ivan
is the elder; he is an intellectual, a student who had lived in
St Petersburg. Alyosha, gentle and loving, far less intellectual, is several years younger; he is living in a monastery

and wearing the habit of a novice and is afraid that Ivan is an atheist. But Ivan tells him he is not. No, he believes in God—only he does not accept the world God has made. Ivan himself has been created—he says—with a mind which works in three dimensions. He has to understand and approve with his reason. Some of the world he not only understands but loves; he keeps coming back to 'the little sticky leaves in spring', which seem to him a sign of love and purpose and life. But much of the world Ivan sees is full of cruelty which he can neither excuse nor understand. He tells Alyosha horrible stories of cruelty to children and then he asks: Would you build a world which had to include the tears of one child beating its breast with its tiny fist in an agony of desertion and despair, tortured by its own parents? And Alyosha has to say he would not. But there is one Being —Alyosha breaks in—who can forgive and reconcile everything. At this point, Ivan, without answering directly, tells his brother the story of the Grand Inquisitor, a story he has imagined as the plot for a long religious poem, a poem he has not written, and never will write.

The scene is Spain, early in the sixteenth century, when the Inquisition was at its most active. In Seville, there has just taken place a great ceremony in which almost a hundred heretics have been burnt alive. That was yesterday. Today, after fifteen hundred years, Christ has come to earth again and is walking among the people. They know at once who he is. Light and power shine from his eyes. The blind see, the lame walk; there is the corpse of a little girl of seven, covered with flowers, on its way to burial; when he speaks to her she sits up with a rose in her hand and smiles. And at that moment the Grand Inquisitor passes. He is an old man of almost ninety but still tall and erect. He too knows at once who this is, makes a sign to the guard and they lay their hands on him and take him. There is no need for a Judas.

That night the Grand Inquisitor visits the prisoner in his cell. He begins to reproach the prisoner. Why has he come back? He had no right to add anything to what he had said before. 'For fifteen hundred years', the Inquisitor goes on, 'we have been trying to put right all that you left undone. You gave men that terrible gift of freedom, but fortunately you also gave us the power to loose and to bind. And we have used that power to give men what they need far more than freedom – all that you refused to give them when that wise and dread spirit asked you those three questions in the desert. They were profound and searching questions – and you gave the wrong answers. You would not turn stones into bread – but it is bread people want. You refused to buy the people with bread because that would be a kind of compulsion; you left them instead the freedom to follow you or reject you. But they do not want freedom. They want certainty; they want a creed, an authority that will tell them exactly what they must do – and yet will forgive them when they do not. They want a creed supported by miracle and mystery – a creed that all will accept blindly, so that they can all be alike – a creed that is backed by dominion over the kingdoms of the earth.

'It was not only', the Inquisitor goes on, 'the purchasing power of bread that you rejected; you would not buy the people with miracle either. You would not fling yourself from the Temple nor come down from the Cross. You rejected the kingdoms of this world as well – and still in the name of naked freedom. We have accepted both the kingdoms and the miracles; we realize that men are weak and idle and silly and are terrified of having to think for themselves. We have pity on them and make things easy. We give them bread; we give them miracles; we give them mystery in worship; we tell them what to believe; we give them firm rule, certainty, content. All this we do in your name – but I know I am fighting against you. I am on the side of that wise and dread spirit. I am too merciful to give them freedom. Your freedom leads only to bloodshed, confusion, the tower of Babel, in the end to slavery and misery. But we give them peace and order, happiness under an easy yoke. And our way is for thousands of millions. Only a few can attain the perfection you demand. So tomorrow I shall burn you.'

There was a long silence. The prisoner had listened intently all this time, looking gently into the Inquisitor's face. He made no reply and the Inquisitor longed for him to say something. Suddenly he approached the old man in silence and kissed him on his aged, bloodless lips. The old man shuddered. He went to the door, opened it, and said: 'Go and come no more.' The prisoner went out into the dark alleys of the town.

That is a much abridged version of Ivan's parable. It is Ivan's parable, please note, not Dostoevsky's; Ivan is someone in Dostoevsky's dream, but then so is Alyosha, and what Alyosha thinks is as much Dostoevsky as what Ivan thinks. Alyosha goes back to his monastery, sad but loving. 'How can you live, with such a Hell in your heart?' he asks Ivan. Ivan replies, with a cold smile, that there is a strength to endure everything. It is an arrogant, self-sufficient reply, not in keeping with the end of his parable. Ivan, who hates cruelty, cannot be on the side of the Inquisitor's methods, but he does give the impression of sympathizing with his arguments, and then, with a twist at the end, turns them upside down.

At one stage, Alyosha says that it is only the Church of Rome that follows the Inquisitor's line; it is not so with the Orthodox Church. Here of course he is wrong; the difference between churches is only a matter of degree. Every organized body of professing Christians has in some degree answered the three temptations in the desert in the Inquisitor's way, not the Prisoner's. Ivan is right not to accept thas point. It is clear that Ivan knows the classical arguments about evil—that the world would not be perfect unless it were *full* and it would not be full unless there was everything in it, even evil; that you could not know light unless there was darkness and so on. But he dismisses such arguments in a breath; all the knowledge in the world, he says, all the fullness, all the harmony and balance, are not worth the tears of one tortured child.

Ivan wants a perfect world in which there is no pain. He perceives, I think, that freedom means freedom to be cruel and he is on the point of saying that he would give up freedom for a world without cruelty. But he cannot bring himself to say it. It is not only that the Inquisitor must be ruthless in order to suppress freedom, but that Ivan cannot acquiesce in the Inquisitor's aim — a mindless uneducated people with no will of their own, who obediently do and think and believe as they are told. Cold and intellectual though he is, at the last he is on the prisoner's side. But he is too impatient for any gradual method. Not for him to toil at changing the factory acts or raising funds to find one child a happy foster home. All he can do is to reject the world, to hand back, as he says, his ticket.

But we, on the other hand, are trying to find some way of living with a freedom that is too big for us, of coming to terms with a perfection we cannot achieve. We are trying to look at the paradox in all its aspects. Let us end this interlude, in which Ivan has expressed in dramatic form the dangers of freedom. Let us go back to the main argument and the difficulties that arise if the teaching of the gospels is applied to the use of force.

4

The Other Cheek

I FORCE AND VIOLENCE

In the gospels, the theme of riches and poverty is constantly recurring. Force is less central. It appears most often not in the negative form – Do not use force – but in the positive form – Do forgive. The background of the Roman state is accepted; soldiers are told not to grumble about their pay, there are judges who will enforce the payment of debts and there is Jewish law with its often harsh sanctions. The state is taken for granted and of the Law nothing is to pass away. But something much more is required of the disciples of Jesus; they are to submit to the state but in their personal relations they must forgive unto seventy times seven, they must turn the other cheek. Anyone who embarks on the new life of Christianity must abjure the use of force, at least for his own aggrandizement or for revenge.

But at once we come up against our old difficulty. There *is* evil in the world. If we do not fight it, we are at its mercy. And what about the protection of others? Is a man to stand by and see his wife injured or ravished? Is he not to protect his child? Suppose the Good Samaritan had arrived while the robbers were actually attacking their victim, what should he have done? Do we turn the other cheek on behalf of the helpless victim of assault? And these personal problems are enormously multiplied as soon as you begin to consider what is to be expected of a Christian state or what is the duty of an individual in a state no longer Christian.

The Church has been trying for two thousand years to define the proper use of force, limiting it where possible, trying to preserve – even in the midst of strife – an intention to forgive in the end. St Augustine tried to reconcile perfectionism with necessity, arguing that judicial punishments were necessary, that there must be soldiers, that there was a distinction between 'counsels' of perfection which men *should* obey and 'commands' which they *must*. No state of any size has ever doubted that *some* force is needed if it is to perform its function. Internally – to take an extreme case within fairly recent memory – hardly anyone would question the duty of the state to restrain a person who has enticed children away from affectionate parents and murdered them, merely for excitement and to satisfy his own lust for power and importance.[1] Before separate nation-states arose, it was usually not difficult in Christendom to reach some kind of general agreement as to what was the proper use of force by individuals. Even since the coming of nation-states, there has been a good deal of agreement on what is murder and what is legitimate self-defence. But it has been much more difficult to limit violence between nation-states.

Let us get rid of a few preliminary points. I use 'force' to mean any method of compelling a person or a body of persons to do something they would not otherwise do. 'Force' includes economic sanctions, strikes and satyāgrāhā, but these are not in themselves 'physical force', though they often lead to it. Physical force may be held in reserve and not actually used. Force is not just legal or legitimate violence; it may be used legally or illegally. 'Violence' is physical force in action and also carries an implication of mere aggression, of being inflicted for its own sake rather than as a means of direct persuasion. Perhaps the victim has refused to comply and then violence is used to fulfil a threat and thus perhaps induce the next victim to submit at once; perhaps it is used indiscriminately – blowing up a shop or a public house to convince a government that you are in earnest. It is force that is used when a criminal is arrested and goes quietly; it is physical force that is used if he resists and has to be overpowered. It is physical force if burglars tie a householder to a chair but violence if they stun him with a blow on the head.

There is one old attitude to force which I want to condemn and one more recent. The old depended on regarding 'soul' and 'body' as utterly separable; you could break a man on the wheel or tear his joints and ligaments on the rack and yet save his soul. It arose from treating a metaphor as something real. It is impossible in thought and speech to avoid making some distinction between the physical body and something that *I* may call the soul or spirit and *you* call mind or individual existence, but to make the distinction so sharp as the Middle Ages did, and to combine it with an unquestioning certainty about the nature of eternity, led to barbarous tortures and cruel executions. No one today who was wholly sane could feel so certain of the nature of death and what follows it as to destroy or torment the body for the sake of benefit to the spirit after death. The body he knows to exist and can see; the spirit is intimately linked to the body, and manifestly capable of being harmed by damage to the body. However ardently he believes that the spirit will exist after death, he cannot know the exact nature of its existence. And for its possible benefit in that state to torture the temple it inhabits here on earth is altogether repugnant. I refer to this ancient horror—a deep reproach to Christendom—not because it now needs combating, but because I think historically it has had some part in our attitude to war, to which I shall come back in a moment. But first, that other dangerous fallacy, the recent one.

It has appeared in the last twenty years or so and its origin is partly in Algeria, partly in the United States. 'Violence is beautiful' its exponents say; most of them have been influenced by the writings of Frantz Fanon.[2] Fanon, a French-speaking black doctor from the Caribbean, went with the French army to Algeria where he was so sickened by what he saw that he went over to the Algerian side. He then experienced a sense of release rather like a religious conversion. His sympathies had been with the Algerians even when he was still with the French – and to be engaged in a cruel war and to feel you are on the wrong side would make any man unhappy. He cast off that burden when he joined the Algerians and found satisfaction in comradeship and shared danger and in complete dedication to a cause. Many before have had such an experience in war.

Fanon went much further. It was not just the pleasures of excitement and danger, or of comradeship, or of total commitment; it was violence itself, the act of killing, that was a cleansing bath, that brought total release. And as a result of that experience he came to preach the cult of violence as something good in itself. The humiliation and suffering inflicted on black people by white could only be purged, he claimed, by killing a white person; only by this means could a black man make himself an equal and recover his lost self-respect, his sense of a real identity of his own. Nothing was of value unless won by violence; no concession freely granted should be accepted, because it would be worth nothing.

This doctrine, which has roots in Hegel and Nietzsche, was expressed by Fanon with an eloquence and sophistication that helped to mask its essential barbarism. It starts from the simple philosophy of *Animal Farm* – two legs bad, four legs good. It obliterates the uniqueness of every individual; all is lost in identity with the group. The other group, the enemy, is for the moment identifiable as white – and is to be killed regardless of individual guilt or innocence. This seems to envisage permanent and indiscriminate racial war and is bad enough – but the idea that nothing is good unless seized by violence is destructive of all society. No contract should be observed if freely negotiated; no obligation should be met unless there is a threat of violence. No association larger than a pirate ship can be run for long on these lines. What will happen to the new society that arises when the whites are all killed? It will either disintegrate into anarchy or be held together by pure terror under a dictator.

Fanon saw horrible cruelty in Algeria; his anger and revulsion at the wrongs of slavery and all that followed slavery mounted to a climax, an ecstasy of hate. That his utterly destructive doctrine was a response to a long and enduring evil does not make it any less a perversion of thought and of language. To kill a man in war may bring an immediate release from tension amounting to pleasure. That may be due to relief that he has not killed you. But unless that is the case, pleasure in killing is an animal reaction from the depths of evolutionary history or a primitive assertion of infantile triumph. That that kind of pleasure happens is a psychological fact; it may be artistically true to portray such an emotion—but to say it is beautiful is a distortion of the meaning of words. It is not; it is ugly.

It has even been argued that violence should be acceptable to Christians because Jesus 'accepted' violence when he accepted death on the Cross. But this again is an utter confusion. There are things for which a man ought to be ready to die; a martyr's death is glorious. But though the martyr may forgive his executioner and even his judge, what they do remains ugly. It is the martyr's courage and fidelity and his readiness to forgive that are beautiful. But the slogan 'violence is beautiful' has caught on and persisted among people who have been made desperate by poverty and neglect and among others who on their behalf are rebels against a society they regard as altogether false and selfish.

Part of what the followers of Fanon are in revolt against is conventional society's glorification of war. To a considerable extent, this glorification is a thing of the past. But, at least until 1914, and even to some extent today, the societies of Western Europe have done honour to the profession of arms. This needs explanation in societies which have till lately professed to be Christian and which historically are the fragmented remnants of Christendom. It enshrines, I think, several elements. The virtues of a soldier in war *are* noble; courage, self-sacrifice for comrades, cheerfulness under hardship, fidelity to a cause, are all truly to be admired. Even in peace, the soldier has put himself permanently at the disposal of others and has declared himself ready to give his life for their protection. Particularly in the British tradition, he has not been supposed to fight for his own benefit but as an instrument of national policy. He has been supposed faithfully to carry out orders given him by the representatives of the nation. And that separation of soul and body, that certainty of life after death, to which I have already referred, have helped people to endure the death of their sons, to cluster round the War Memorial and sing hymns, to contemplate the continuance of war as an institution. This leads to perhaps the most important element, the idea that there can be a just war.

2 THE JUST WAR

Since the time of St Thomas Aquinas, Europe has had a clear doctrine of the circumstances in which a war can be just and therefore acceptable to a Christian conscience. The conditions for a just war that Aquinas laid down were designed to prevent unnecessary wars and to limit the worst features of war. Every effort, he wrote, must have been made to find a peaceful solution before resort is had to war. The cause for which the war is fought must be just, and the aims of the warring power must remain just while the war continues. The methods employed must be just. The peace with which the war ends must be just and the results for humanity better than if the war had not been fought. It follows that there must be some reasonable chance of success.

That may sound a little like saying that a war is just if it *is* just. But, up to a point, those principles did lead to some limitation of the worst aspects of war, and in particular, to some definition of just and unjust methods. There was, in the years before 1914, some international agreement on the rights of neutrals at sea, on the rights of civilians, of prisoners of war and of the sick and wounded. It was contrary to international law to use poison of any kind or unmoored floating mines. It was agreed as a general principle that 'the troops alone carry on war while the rest of the nation remain in peace'. Most of these agreements were broken in the war of 1914, but until that war it was reasonable to hope for increasing limitation at least of *indiscriminate* means of waging war.

Those attempts at some international definition of how war might be justly waged broke down. The concept of Christendom was dying; Christian beliefs were losing ground to a philosophy of aggressive self-hood; above all, national sovereignty was absolute. The Europe of Christendom had broken up into nation-states and they had so far taken only the first feeble steps towards a system of agreed international law. There were no means of enforcing what had been agreed.

In the titanic struggle of 1914–18, each side believed it was fighting for existence. Poison gas was used, merchant and passenger ships were sunk without warning and with no means of escape for crew and passengers, open towns were shelled or bombed, not to compel them to surrender but to destroy them. There was an end to the idea that only troops were at war; it was total war, the whole nation against the whole nation, and the aim was to break the will of the civil population. The final blow to the idea of the just war came in the Second World War with the nuclear bomb, but long before that was dropped on Japan, 'just methods' had been abandoned. Whole cities were being methodically destroyed by bombing from the air. Destruction was indiscriminate. And it had become impossible to picture a war of which the cost in lives and misery would not exceed the benefits.

Is there any point then in talking about a just war? Does

it not appear that, in this respect at least, St Thomas's attempt to modify the stark opposition between the Sermon on the Mount and life in a national state has broken down? Indeed, the whole-hearted pacifist might argue that the attempt at reconciliation had done harm by allowing people to think that there could be a war that was just. Up to a point, the answer to these questions is yes. It has broken down, though the conditions for a just war are still useful criteria when considered in relation to a rebellion. And the aim of reconciliation after force has been used is still valid. But the fault does not lie with Aquinas's thinking. It is due to two simple facts. Modern methods of war are so powerful that they are bound to be indiscriminate and therefore unjust, while since 1914 no powerful nation has been prepared to trust any other to keep an agreement. It is no longer possible to visualize a 'just war' even between nations with virtually no industrial power of their own, because no such war can be isolated. Industrial nations would side with one or the other of the combatants and supply them with arms, perhaps not nuclear but still indiscriminate. There would be bombing from the air, incendiary bombs, napalm, rockets.

Does it follow from this that the only consistent course open to a professing Christian is outright pacifism? Once again, the answer is inextricably involved with the whole paradox of impracticable perfection. But let me make some preliminary points. I respect the few I have known who, being of military age, felt they could in no circumstances take part in killing others and so dug vegetables in the war of 1939. Yet they are without exception people to whom Hitler's regime was repugnant. Nazism was surely as near absolute evil as humanity can get. It added to the mindless stupidity of *wishing* to exterminate an intelligent, industrious and kindly people the cold-blooded organization to carry it out; it picked out for its service the worst of a whole population and corrupted the weakest; it set about the task of corruption with the same deadly concentration that it devoted to massacre. It had to be destroyed—and I find it hard to see how anyone could will that end without willing the means. To insist that I must dig potatoes, while others are killing and being killed in order to achieve an end I want to see—that is something I find hard to stomach. There is evil; there are times when it has to be fought. Indeed, I do not see how there can be a just society unless there are people ready to fight to keep it just, whether as police or as soldiers. You may have to take a share in that fighting. You can still forgive when it is over.

But though thinking about the just war has led me back to the stark opposition between Christian teaching and any kind of war that is possible today, it is not altogether unfruitful, even at this stage. The most important of St Thomas's conditions were that there should be a just peace and that the world should be a better place when the war was over—conditions which have certainly not been fulfilled after the two world wars of my lifetime. Why do wars occur? Sometimes because there was an unjust peace. I do not think it is true that the evil of Hitler arose wholly from an unjust peace—the fact that there was no forgiveness after the First War—but I have no doubt it was one of the reasons. And there can be no doubt at all that the questions we should always be asking are: Is it a just peace? Is it a peace likely to lead to war or rebellion? Are we taking a just line about oil or fishing or pollution?

3 THE JUST REBELLION

The just rebellion also was something Aquinas discussed. In his time, of course, the nation-state was only just beginning to emerge. The kind of state which he had in mind was nearer to Athens or Florence or Venice than to France or England, but the principles are much the same. His argument recalls the famous saying of St Augustine: 'Without justice, what are states but bands of robbers on a large scale?' (Remota justitia, quid regna nisi magna latrocinia?) The 'justice' that makes a state something better must be some degree of internal agreement – some feeling that the division of functions and goods is fair and that those who rule do so in the interest of those who are ruled. It was Plato's idea of a just state that every man should perform his proper function – and the function of the rulers was to rule for the benefit of the people – like a sheep-dog for the sheep. Paul had added that the head must feel pain when the foot is injured. And Aquinas went on from this to say: 'a tyrannical regime is not just, since it is not directed towards the common good but towards the private good of the ruler ... and therefore the overthrow of such a regime does not partake of the nature of sedition, unless perhaps the violence involved is so extreme that the mass of the governed suffer more harm from the upheaval than from the rule of the tyrant. A tyrant is rather himself guilty of sedition, inasmuch as he fosters discord and strife among the people so that he can more safely dominate them.' And as Lord Ramsey of Canterbury has pointed out, that is the doctrine of the American Declaration of Independence, which says: 'Whenever any Form of Government becomes destructive of these ends' – that is, the proper ends of humanity – 'it is the right of the People to alter or abolish it, and to institute a new Government, laying its foundation on such principles and organizing its powers in such forms as then shall seem most likely to effect their safety and happiness.'[3]

A just rebellion is therefore possible in theory and the conditions are much the same as for the just war. All other means must have been tried and reform must have been irretrievably refused. The aims must be just in the first place and must continue to be just. The methods must be just and there must be some hope of success. There can be few rebellions which have fulfilled all the conditions exactly; by the end, they have seldom preserved the purity of the aims with which they began; there has seldom been much mercy for those who previously refused peaceful reform. Nonetheless, it may be possible to hope for some degree of fulfilment. Today, the most relevant condition is perhaps the chance of success. In Hungary and Czechoslovakia, elected governments have been removed by a foreign power and it seems possible – though I have no first-hand knowledge – that most of the population regard their government as a tyranny. I am doubtful whether that is so in Spain. But in none of these cases does it seem likely that a rebellion would have the least chance of success.

South Africa is the clearest case I know in the modern world of a state in which rebellion would be justified if there was a chance of success and if the methods could be prevented from becoming indiscriminate. A minority of less than one fifth holds all the power in the state. They rule primarily for their own good, openly distinguishing between the two populations, giving the majority no say in public affairs and trying to create divisions among the majority to make their own rule more lasting. In Aquinas's sense, it is the rulers who are seditious. It is a country in which the rights which have been internationally proclaimed proper for human beings are not merely ignored – as they are in many countries – but are explicitly denied by law to the majority of the citizens on grounds of their race. As the trial of Mandela showed convincingly, peaceful means of reform have been proposed again and again and have always been refused. It is incidentally a country for which Britain has some responsibility, because of the extent of our trade with South Africa and our investments there, also because of the 'liberal' peace made by Britain after the South African War, which put the black population in the hands of the whites. But here too the chances of a rebellion being directly successful – that is, of overthrowing the government – are clearly remote.

It is sometimes argued that in South Africa a sacrificial rebellion might be justified; that is to say, a rebellion which was known to have no hope of direct success but which might, by the loss of life involved, draw the attention of the world to the situation and force the South African government to make reforms. It is a fact that the South African government has often shown itself sensitive to the opinion of what were once called the liberal democracies – but never to the extent of conceding anything that threatens white rule. On that, a majority of the whites is adamant. We may of course expect action meant to persuade the rest of the world that there is an intention of reform. Indeed, we have been seeing such demonstrations for the last twenty years. And certainly there is a desire to avoid direct confrontation with other African states. But on essential points it seems most unlikely that there will be any giving way except by compulsion.

A sacrificial rebellion, to be successful, would have to produce a determined and almost unanimous reaction from the most powerful states in the world. This is hard to imagine. The illegal government of Rhodesia has lasted ten years in the face of the professed disapproval of most of the world; South Africa would be far more difficult to coerce. No combination of African states can – in the last months of 1975 – be a serious military threat to South Africa. Neither Russia, China nor the U.S.A. seems likely to engage in full-scale military adventures at such a distance, still less Britain or France. The U.K.'s trade with South Africa is an important part of an economy which – to put it at the lowest – has no surplus it can lose without making a sacrifice that would demand altruistic leadership of a much higher order than is discernible. France supplies a large part of South Africa's arms. Altogether, there seems little chance of a sacrificial rebellion in South Africa having much international effect.

Such judgments seem to imply that a warlike attack on South Africa by an external power is desirable. On the contrary, the general conclusion about war still holds. However much one may dislike the South African regime, no detached person can seriously believe that a war against South Africa could be anything but indiscriminate and therefore unjust, causing terrible suffering to both black and white, probably much greater suffering than the black majority endure at present.

South Africa is an example of the kind of problem that continually presents itself to anyone with sympathy for human suffering who tries to judge with a clear mind. The intellect presents a cold and usually depressing picture of what is likely to happen; the heart indignantly rejects it. And there is the added complication that to state in public what seems only too likely to happen is often to make it more likely that it will. It would be out of place in this argument to formulate the deep forebodings with which I regard the future of South Africa. In any case, to any judgment based on human probability there is the reservation that the Holy Spirit may inspire someone to change the whole situation.

I am, however, still convinced of the validity of two sentences which appeared in the report of a working-party of the British Council of Churches (of which I was chairman) in 1970. They ran as follows: 'Those who are themselves in comfort and security cannot urge armed rebellion on others who would thereby face death or life imprisonment. Nor can they preach patient endurance they do not have to bear.' But I could not now subscribe to the sentence that followed: 'But we cannot sincerely withhold support from those who have decided to face the certain suffering involved in rebellion.' It seems to me now that that is very near to 'urging armed rebellion'. And there is something I find increasingly distasteful about 'supporting' something in which one takes no risks.

4   PASSIVE RESISTANCE

But if rebellion in South Africa, though justified on all other grounds, has no chance of success, what about some form of passive resistance?[4] This is still force—compelling someone to do something he would not otherwise do. It is not physical force. Mahatma Gandhi made this method famous, using for it the Sanskritic word satyāgrāhā, which means 'truth force'. For him it was something positive, a spiritual force, not a mere lever or form of coercion; the truth, the just cause, would prevail, he thought, when the attention of insensitive rulers was drawn to it with sufficient vigour. It was incidentally an adaptation of a very ancient Indian custom, by which a suppliant would take up his station on the doorstep of the person from whom he sought a favour and fast till it was granted. It is still force – making someone do something he otherwise would not.

It is reasonable to ask of passive resistance – as of rebellion – whether all other means have been tried. Again, can motives and methods be kept pure? Even the enormous prestige of Gandhi in India was unable to keep his first movement non-violent. There was the famous episode of Chauri Chaura when a police station – with its Indian staff alive inside – was burnt down by a mob whose leaders had lost control. Outbreaks of unintended violence led Gandhi to believe his first movement in India had been a 'Himalayan blunder'. But it would be unreasonable to regard the danger of such outbreaks as a final objection to the use of passive resistance; it might still be less violent than a rebellion that did not even pay lip-service to non-violence. The real objection is that it has little chance of success against a ruthless government which feels its vital interests are affected.

That point is made clearly by the early history of satyāgrāhā in South Africa, where Gandhi first made use of it. This was in 1906, when he invoked it against an ordinance which sought to impose pass-laws on Indians in the Transvaal. He headed a deputation to London, where he received a favourable hearing from the Secretary of State for the Colonies, who refused his consent to the ordinance. But a year later the Transvaal became self-governing and the ordinance was restored. For some years the struggle continued, Gandhi spending several periods in prison and scoring some successes, usually because General Smuts was still ready to listen to advice from London. There was a Liberal Government in London, and sympathy for the Indians of the Transvaal demanded no sacrifice by British taxpayers. But years later, when Smuts was defeated, there was an end to the influence of a distant liberalism. An attempt was made to revive satyāgrāhā in Natal in the early fifties but it was firmly repressed and powers were taken to deal with it far more severely. They have hardly been needed; the certainty of unflinching repression and the knowledge that the South African government will not yield to peaceful demonstration combine to make passive resistance a course that only an occasional martyr is ready to adopt.

Satyāgrāhā was a different matter in India. It was the avowed policy of the Government of India to hand over power gradually to Indians and the dispute was about the speed at which this should happen, not the principle. The British in India did not regard India as their permanent home. And the last word lay with people far away in London who were responsible to an electorate that did not look on India as a vital interest. White South Africans take a very different view of white supremacy. No one, so far as I know, has even suggested trying passive resistance in Hungary or Czechoslovakia.

Thinking about satyāgrāhā leads to a rather similar conclusion about a limited use of violence in small doses. This too works only against a government already half converted. In the fifties and early sixties, the three British parties were in very broad agreement on the principle of decolonization in Africa; they differed in emphasis and particularly about speed. In this situation, limited violence was an effective accelerator. In the Gold Coast, Nyasaland, and Northern Rhodesia, limited violence produced stern declarations about the impossibility of dealing with the leaders of such movements, followed shortly by negotiations which culminated in independence. In Kenya, more violence was employed than was needed.

Palestine, Cyprus, Malaya, underline the point. This historical pattern has contributed to the cult of violence but does not affect the essential truth that pushing against a swing door is not the same as butting against a brick wall.

5   IN PRAISE OF HYPOCRISY

Satyāgrāhā is not likely to work in South Africa; it would not have worked against Hitler. It was useful against the British in India because many of its aims were in accordance with what the British had themselves announced as their intentions. It worked, in short, against a nation of hypocrites who were inclined to postpone putting their good resolutions into effect.

Let us pause for a brief hymn in praise of hypocrisy. I am thinking more of public than of personal hypocrisy, but even in the personal field I am not sure the hypocrite has had a fair press. Tartuffe and Pecksniff are the great models; let us consider Pecksniff. Of course it is odious to make up to an old man for the sake of his money, to attempt to marry a young girl for hers, to dismiss a faithful servant for finding one out. What we see in Dickens is the harsh contrast between the man's lofty professions and what he does, and most readers – and perhaps Dickens – take it for granted that Pecksniff is aware all the time of his own motives and only pretends to profess virtue. This is early Dickens, not notable for subtlety. But in real life, is it not far more likely that Pecksniff would deceive himself before anyone else? Would he not really intend to live up to the lofty sentiments he expresses, to persuade himself that old Mr Chuzzlewit – quite independently of his money – really needs protection? And would he not be less detestable than Jonas Chuzzlewit, who with everything he says has to convey his conviction that everyone else is as selfish as himself – as narrow, as mean, as determined to get the better of others? I am not sure about this; they are both horrid people. But it does seem to me that even, on the personal

level, life would be far more abrasive without the emollient
of the mild hypocrisy involved in courtesy. And there is
much to be said for living in a society where it is fashionable
to pay lip-service to altruism rather than one where no one
dares profess any motive but self-seeking for fear of being
thought a prig.

George Orwell once said that every humanitarian was a
hypocrite;[5] he meant, I suppose, that such a man as Lord
Shaftesbury of the Factory Acts could not live up to his own
ideals. Surely Lord Shaftesbury would have been the first
to admit it – as would anyone who has given any thought
to the impracticable perfectionism of the gospels. Let us go
further; anyone who seeks to be a Christian is bound to be
a hypocrite, if that means to accept a target he knows he
cannot live up to. But even hypocrisy in the ordinary sense,
that is deliberately pretending to be better than you are,
seems to me preferable to what Iago called hypocrisy
against the devil – or pretending to be worse than you are.
It is better to pay tribute to virtue than to vice.

A terrible spiral operates between public statements and
private. Let a judge or a Member of Parliament utter a
prejudiced and intolerant pronouncement about a racial
minority and many of the public will begin to say worse and
before long gangs will hunt them in the streets. In a country
whose leaders talk only of prices and wages, and assume a
cynical self-interest in everyone else, every group will
come to do the same, and the state will indeed become a
gang of robbers. The justice which makes a true state
depends on a network of forbearance and restraint and
respect for the function and position of others. And it is no
bad thing to pay lip-service to virtues which hold society
together.

There is a more profound point too. 'Not what thou
art but what thou wouldst be does God consider ... '[6] and
you may come in time really to want to be what you say
you are trying to be.

6 THE VISION OF CO-INHERENCE

Ivan's Grand Inquisitor put the view that man was not fit for freedom, which he neither wanted nor deserved. It is the fascist view. It is the direct opposite—as the Inquisitor saw—of the message of the Incarnation. And the brief glance we have just given to Aquinas's great attempt to limit and define the use of force might be thought to confirm the Grand Inquisitor's opinion. We have terribly abused our freedom. From the moment when Constantine became a Christian, the paradox of a state that used force at every turn but professed a religion of non-violence has been at the heart of Europe. From Augustine to Aquinas and Dante, minds of great power, inspired by nothing less than the love of God and of man, tried to build an intellectual and political system that would resolve the paradox. Their starting point was the just state conceived by Plato, in which, as in the Hindu ideal of the state, every man performs his allotted function. But Augustine turned Plato's austere Republic—an essentially aristocratic republic which despised the common man—into something far warmer and more glorious, the City of God upon earth, which was an imperfect copy of the City of God in heaven, knitted together by the love of God for man and by man's common sonship. It was a noble vision, in which the spiritual bond between men—whose manhood has been taken up into God—was humbly and earthily represented by the network of feudal and ecclesiastical obligations and responsibilities—upward and downward—culminating in Pope and Emperor. Fidelity was due to a feudal superior, justice and paternal care to dependents. Within that framework of co-inherence emerged St Thomas's great attempt to define in intellectual terms the limits of what was permissible to man—man who had fallen so infinitely far short of the perfection enjoined on him.

It is easy enough to make fun of that structure, as Gib-

bon did, as Voltaire did—though far from easy to do it
with the style and wit of either. It fell hopelessly short of its
ideals. Even where it made slow progress—as it did before
1914 towards rules of war that might be more just—that
progress was swept away by human selfishness and blind-
ness. Today it will seem to most Europeans a dream as
irrelevant as the Islamic concept of the Khalif as the
Shadow of God upon earth. A dream—but it was nonetheless noble and to remember it may help us to find something
that will take its place. Of course we cannot go back. Of
course we cannot find any solution on those lines. Certainly
not, but the spirit in which that vision was conceived is
relevant to the search for a new order. We live in a time
when the Spirit is groaning and travailing to bring something new to birth. So for that matter did Paul. So did
Augustine. So did Aquinas. The times change but certain
profound oppositions and relations are constant. Rights
balance duties; freedom carries responsibilities; darkness
cannot understand light.

Let me end this chapter once again, with a question.
Do you think that the failure of that vision reinforces the
Grand Inquisitor's view? Must we refuse freedom? Ivan
flinched from that conclusion. The Grand Inquisitor
flinched. He sent the prisoner away instead of burning
him. The prisoner went out into the dark alleys of the town.

And it was night.

Second Interlude:
Light and Darkness

Turn back to the picture of the prisoner – Christ returned to earth – going out into the dark alleys of the town. I added: 'And it was night' – because the scene brings to mind that intensely dramatic moment in the Gospel of St John when Judas went out into the night. The heart was heavy in his breast; in his ears were the words: 'What you are going to do, do quickly.' He went out into the night, away from the light of supper with his friends and away from the light of his Lord's presence. Light is one of the great themes of that gospel, and it is on that gospel I want to dwell in this second interlude, thinking of it for the moment as a work of art.

The themes which spring to mind are Light and Life, Glory, Love – and the Eternity of the Word which was in the Beginning. The glory is realized through sacrifice, for it is in this gospel that Jesus so often speaks of himself as being glorified when he is lifted up by the shameful and agonizing death that he foresaw. But in a kind of counterpoint with these themes are certain earthly – indeed, earthy – symbols. Wine, water and bread are the three great symbols but there are others too – wind, which is the breath of the Spirit; the grain of corn, which is Life about to be renewed; the sheep-fold and the vine – and to think of that gospel is to think of other earthy details, water-pots, fish and a fire of coals, spittle and the stink of death. I have no doubt at all that one artist was behind the whole work as author and sometimes editor, grouping the discourses he puts into the mouth of Jesus around the seven signs which he has chosen to emphasize out of many other works. The signs he has chosen illustrate the themes of Light and Life and Joy by the symbols of wine and water and bread.

I picture[1] – and here I am less certain – that artist as one of a group, disciples of John the son of Zebedee, disciples who had often heard their master talk of all that he remembered, who had heard him comment on historical points in the synoptic gospels, who had sometimes heard him speak with the tongue of that fiery young man who had once been called the Son of Thunder and, on other occasions, with the tenderness that sometimes comes in old age to a man of action after a life of service and self-discipline. That artist was soaked in the teaching of his master and had something of that mixed temperament, impulsive, choleric and loving. But he was a teacher in his own right too. Perhaps he read what he had written to his friends and asked for their comments. Perhaps he read it to his master; perhaps he dedicated his book to his master's name after his death. What I am sure of is that it is one man's work and that if any piece of literature in the world is inspired, it is this. And I am confident that the author was in touch with someone who had known Jesus.

But I am concerned now with the theme of Light contrasted with Darkness. The three synoptic gospels were written to collect the teachings and doings of Jesus while they were still remembered. The main purpose of this gospel, on the other hand, was to define certain aspects of belief. It is really a creed in dramatic form, cast in the form of a gospel. It was aimed at heresies – errors in belief – and it provides an answer to all the great heresies. But because the truth is many-sided, and because a heresy is always an insistence on one aspect of the truth and the error lies in excluding other aspects, John's gospel brings us back again and again to the very paradox with which we started – and that most emphatically in the contrast between Light and Darkness.

He wanted to combat the idea that Light and Life were a matter of special knowledge, something only attainable by a few people who had been properly instructed; that was part of what the Gnostics believed. Sometimes it was secret knowledge that would save them and it could only be passed on under an oath of secrecy, with a password, as in masonry. But it would be misleading to speak as though there was one Gnostic system. There were a great many sects, over several centuries, with very varied systems. Common to them all was a belief that the created world was something evil from which man should try to escape. Not all Gnostics professed to be Christian but for those who did it followed that Christ's appearance in an evil world was an intervention from outside, that he had in no sense become part of the natural order.

This above all the writer of St John wanted to rebut. He wanted to make it clear that God had not only *seemed* to be a man. He wanted to rub in the astounding fact that the Word, the eternal Word – God in action – really had become flesh – real flesh – flesh and blood and bone; He had walked and talked and His friends had touched Him. But the artist must not obscure the sense of otherness, of Holiness, of Eternal Spirit that they had felt. They had all been in awe of Him. And certainly – it had to be admitted – a great deal of His teaching had implied a division between spirit and matter. It was the spirit that counted, He kept saying. On every page, the contrast, the paradox, is there. His presence in the world was a touchstone, dividing good from bad. The world was made by Him and the world received Him not. He had overcome the world yet He loved the world. The poet who wrote this creed in the form of drama trembles constantly on the edge of saying exactly what he has set out to deny, that the world is evil, that flesh is evil – which seems to carry with it the implication that the world was made not by the loving Father whom Jesus addressed but by some other power.

That indeed was part of the teaching of most of the

Gnostics. Later, much more definitely, it was to be part of
the teaching of the Manichaeans. Among the Gnostics, it
took various forms. Some fashioned elaborate myths in
which the material world was created by a demiurge, an
artisan inferior to the Ultimate Creator; sometimes, there
were seven such spirits; sometimes, Satan was one of
them, sometimes the Jehovah of the Old Testament – who
was neither Supreme Being nor Loving Father. These
were all attempts to make sense of a world full of evil as
well as of good. They were flat, hard and unyielding – like
a jig-saw puzzle – quite unlike the organic relations of
reality. The human mind, it seems, has to clamour for
simple answers, to classify, to put things in pigeon-holes. It
is the beginning of thought – but it is deadening if it is
allowed to become the end of thought. And, of course, if
you picture an ultimate Supreme Being, it is no answer to
the problem of evil to suppose that He allowed some inferior
emanation of His power, some servant or agent, to con-
struct an evil world when He was looking the other way;
He cannot escape responsibility by any such device.

It was this that the artist of St John confronted with his
creed, in which he anticipated the formal creeds, asserting
vigorously – and in the end joyously – that the Word was
there from the beginning, that the Word took part in the
Creation, that the Word became flesh and lived among us
and suffered with man and for man; that the Creation in
some mysterious and incomprehensible way was *one* and
good though it included evil. It follows – it seems to me –
from that extraordinary combination of the eternal and the
finite with which John's gospel opens that *all* man's
attempts to create beauty and to understand the divine are
part of the same Creation; all things were made by the Word
and all these interpretations take place by the inspiration of
the Spirit. But Christendom has been slow to perceive that
the Word was at work in Hinduism and Islam, in Shakespeare and Beethoven as well as in Aquinas and Francis,
in Voltaire, in Darwin and Freud as well as in Blake.

Of course, the Spirit has not been present in an equal degree in all these manifestations but nowhere, as I have said, more completely than here in St John's Gospel. The artist who wrote it was an intuitive, a sacramentalist, a poet rather than an intellectual. He does not attempt to explain evil – he records it. He knows it. He had seen it. He had seen it when men came with lanterns and torches and weapons, and in that scene of smoky confusion, went backwards and fell to the ground at the words: 'I am he.' Darkness and light are contrasted once again and in both senses, physical and moral; physically there is light only here and there, flaring in a torch or gleaming from a sword; in the other dimension, there is the horror of the betrayal, the shame of sudden panic – but set against that the memory of that solitary figure before whom both guards and rabble fell back and abased themselves. The light yielded to darkness but was not overcome. There is no reconciliation in intellectual terms. Although it is one Creation, the emphasis is on the contrast within it. And it has been on this contrast that the restless, simplifying minds of mankind have seized and have divided mind from body, darkness from light, emphasizing now one now the other. But both are part of the problem. Neither must be forgotten. There is always opposition but a unity behind it, an ultimate reconciliation.

6

Deny Yourself

Negativity is one of the charges that can fairly be made today against Christianity as a working system of belief, as a way of life. It has, the accuser will say, been hopelessly infected by the dualism of its early opponents, the Gnostics, and has chosen to reject the material creation. Deny yourself, the Master had said, and blessed are the meek, but such a command – it may be argued – runs clean counter to the principles of evolution; plants and animals survive by aggression and why not man? How nasty and brutish was man's life before he set himself to improve it! And that he did by asserting his will to survive. It is by determination, self-assertion, by successful competition, not by meekness, by hard work, not by prayer, that the great scientific discoveries have been made, that pain has been alleviated and disease cured, that vast irrigation systems have increased our crops, that rivers have been harnessed and light and heat brought to our homes. And – my imaginary opponent may continue – even if I accept your premise that there is what you call a 'purpose' in life, it cannot be in accordance with that purpose that we should deny the very principle by which creation is accomplished and refuse to share to the full the goodness of the world we live in. That is the kind of charge a Western materialist might make.

On the other hand, to an Asian or an African it often seems that those who sent missionaries to teach their fathers a religion of self-denial are the very people who to them epitomize selfishness and greed, a neurotic self-

assertion, a restless concern to magnify individual importance. Once again, we preach something we do not believe
and which would destroy our society if we accepted it, but
in practice act in exactly the opposite sense. And the
thoughtful young in the West will argue that, while they
accept it as a duty to share food and other goods with all
men – a duty in which the nation-states of the West have
signally failed – they see no virtue in any self-denial which
does not give direct benefit to someone else. To do your
thing, to realize your own best potential to the full, to
many of them is more important than anything else. How
joyless and negative much of Western Christianity seems!
No one understood it better than Blake:

> And the gates of this Chapel were shut
> And 'Thou shalt not' writ over the door.

Or again:

> Dear mother, dear mother, the Church is cold
> But the Ale-house is healthy and pleasant and warm.

Christianity, they will say, was infected with the dualism it
condemned and overcame; it never threw off the sombre
conviction of the Gnostics that flesh was evil and that it was
the task of man to escape from an evil creation.

Now of course there is truth in this charge. Indeed, it is
true of every religion, as opposed to a philosophy, that its
adherents at some stage and in some degree feel themselves
strangers on earth. Hindu, Buddhist and Muslim as well as
Christian have consequently admired austerity of life. And
some have carried it to extremes. I have talked to Hindus
who have put themselves into a kind of trance and survived,
almost without food, buried under snow in a Himalayan
winter, in one case actually on the ice of a glacier at over
14,000 feet. I could get no impression that this had led to a
growth in spirituality and I think most informed Hindus

would agree that this way is not a way but a dead end. Austerity – I think in all systems – has no value in itself but only as a means to an end. Even in a system so minutely particular as the Hindu about ceremonial purity in matters of washing, eating and drinking, there are those who would understand the famous saying of St Augustine of Hippo – 'Dilige et quod vis fac.' It is generally translated: 'Love and do what you like', but I suspect that it really needs a fuller translation: 'Make a loving choice and then do whatever as a result of that choice you truly desire.' 'Diligo' does mean 'I love' but it also means 'I choose'.

The extremes of Christian austerity were reached by the Desert Fathers from the later part of the third century to the end of the fifth. Like the Hindu hermit whom I met on the glacier, some of the Christian hermits in the desert engaged themselves in forms of bodily denial so extreme that they cannot have been truly a training of the spirit. Their elders those who became leaders when they formed communities, seem to have been well aware of the dangers. Their sayings, teem with assertions that austerity by itself is nothing. There is a tale, for instance, of one who was anxious about the interpretation of a passage in the scriptures. He asked God to reveal the true explanation and – in order to emphasize his question, to bring it to notice as it were, and perhaps, half-consciously, to enforce his demand – he began a fast, eating only once a week. This lasted seventy weeks but no reply was vouchsafed. And then he thought that he would go and ask a brother better informed than himself. He started at once and as he closed the door of his cell, an angel appeared to tell him that his humility in seeking help from his brother had done what seventy weeks of fasting had not – and there and then the angel explained the text.

Again and again there is gentle reproof for those who persist in fasting in the presence of visitors; there is the recurring story of the visitor who goes away thinking that the famed austerity of the desert had been exaggerated, only to discover that he had been entertained with luxuries which the hermit-monks never touched when alone. They are always insisting that it is not what you do but the spirit in which it is done that is important. One of the fathers was approached for counsel by a brother who was tormented by his conscience because he had two gold pieces, which he had put by in case of sickness. 'Shall I keep them?' he asked. 'Yes,' said the elder. The brother went away but he was still tormented. He came back to the elder, who said: 'I knew you wanted to keep them. But you will never have rest till you trust wholly in God.' And there is reproof for a brother visiting another community who tried to impress them by the sharpness of his self-denial.

Yet if the best of them concealed the more extreme of the rigours they imposed on themselves, if all the leaders insisted that austerity had no merit of its own, there can be no question that they had chosen the way of negation. 'The notion of the way of rejection', wrote Charles Williams of the Desert Fathers, ' – of the reduction of both soul and body to as near a state of nothingness under God as might be won – gained strangely on life. The huts, the caves, the pillars of the ascetics did indeed hold those who concentrated on nothing but their relation with God, to whom the whole outer world and (but for one thought) the whole inner world had become temptation.' The movement cannot be precisely dated – no movement of the spirit can – but Anthony, who was certainly one of the first of the desert hermits, seems to have taken to this way of life about A.D. 270, that is, forty years before the Edict of Milan gave Christianity tolerance throughout the West and fifty years before Constantine became sole Emperor. It cannot be said, then, that the migration to the caves and cells of the desert was entirely a movement of protest at Christianity's new respectability. On the other hand, the possibility of martyrdom must have provided a bracing tension and when that tension relaxed men would feel the loss of it and the need to seek perfection by austerity if not by danger. The bifurcation of Christendom is illustrated by the life of

Arsenius, one of the gentlest and sweetest of the recluses, who was tutor to the sons of the Emperor Theodosius and lived in kings' houses till he was forty. He was learned in both Greek and Latin and 'when he was in the palace none wore finer garments than he – and when he was in holy living none was so poorly clad.' To conceal his learning, he would never consent to expound or interpret the Scriptures and when he came to a gathering of brothers in church would try to sit behind a pillar so that he should not be seen. He lived till he was nearly a hundred years old, dying two hundred years after the birth of Anthony.

You may say that the Desert Fathers have little relevance today, but they illustrate in its extreme form that aspect of Christianity which my imaginary opponent is urging as a reproach.[1] They were the earliest Christian monks and represent an important stage in monastic development; they quickly adopted a form of community life, in which the occupants of various scattered cells would meet for worship on Sundays; they developed a doctrine of work, weaving mats and baskets – mechanical work which kept the fingers busy while the spirit was at prayer – and often earned enough to make a contribution to the poor of the nearest town. It is recorded how a certain Lucius refuted a group of monks who claimed that they engaged in unceasing prayer and could not pause to work with their hands, converting them in the end to the value of handiwork. In many ways, then, the Desert Fathers laid the foundations for the rule of St Benedict and its cardinal maxim of work as well as prayer. But there is not much sign at this stage of the belief that the prayers of the monks would perfume and sweeten the secular world.

Now my imaginary opponent – Hobbs, Nobbs, Nokes or Stokes;[2] let us call him Nokes for convenience – is a reasonable man, and so am I. We can agree that extreme physical austerity is not a good way to what we are both dimly striving for. We can also agree not to embark on a discussion of monasticism. Nokes is firmly in the secular world, making motor cars perhaps or growing food. But he has his moments – moments when a piece of music or a child or a tree or a sunset, or simply a kind act, convinces him that there is a timeless dimension which takes him outside the world he knows. Who am I, he will sometimes ask, and wonder dizzily what will become of this fragile identity and all he has learnt when the body has dissolved.

Nokes wants to bring such moments into focus, to relate them to a system of belief that will help him to renew them and to understand them. Yet the services of the Church are for those who have had some instruction and already believe; they are not meant for absolute beginners. And if he turns to, say, *The Imitation of Christ*, perhaps the most widely read of all books of devotion, he will find in the very first chapter an insistence on the vanity of knowledge; he is told to withdraw his heart from the love of visible things and direct his affections to things invisible. He will find it hard to know how to begin on such a course. Indeed, he may well say: 'But so far in my life I have been trying, however imperfectly, to improve myself by learning skills. I have tried to educate myself by drawing out the best that was in me. I have tried to strengthen my character and develop my brain and become a mature person. Was I wrong?' Or if he turns, in the Protestant tradition, to *The Pilgrim's Progress*, he will find a man with a burden of sin on his back, who is wretched till he can get rid of it. But Nokes is a decent enough fellow; he has sometimes had to be tough and stand up for himself – and indeed he would have hardly been able to keep his farm or his factory going if he had not. But he has not done anything that he feels can provoke most justly God's wrath and indignation. He does not feel there is a burden on his back so much as an emptiness at the heart. Where is he to make a beginning?

Nokes has been brought up either with no religious education at all or with a bad one. He and his generation are either absolute beginners or they have been perfunctorily taught about, say, the Garden of Eden, a myth that contains a profound truth, by someone who neither believes its literal truth nor perceives its inner truth. And that is a souring experience. And neither *The Imitation* nor *The Pilgrim's Progress* were written for absolute beginners but for people steeped in belief, for people who have heard the paradoxes of the gospels perhaps daily, and certainly weekly, since their cradles. I will agree with Nokes that the welcome the modern beginner may easily find if he turns to traditional religion may seem singularly bleak and negative.

Now I am quite convinced that there is ultimately no easy way by which Nokes can increase the frequency and intensity of what he calls his 'moments' and relate them to a system of belief. If it is easy, it is bogus. That is to me an axiom. But there is an affirmative approach as well as a negative. Let us, however, first pause a little on the negative way. Its dangers were put in figurative language by Jesus when he spoke of the seven worse devils that an evil spirit would bring to a house that he found swept and garnished. The dangers were seen very clearly by a master of the negative way, the author of *The Cloud of Unknowing*. The purpose of that treatise is to teach a disciple, who has determined to make perfection his life's work, how to attain communion with God by emptying himself of all discursive thought and all images of created things; he must attain abstraction from sense and from ordinary human knowledge and beat upon this 'cloud of unknowing', in which he feels nothing but 'a naked intent unto God', with 'a sharp dart of longing love', using one word only, perhaps the word 'love', and saying it over and over again. 'Strip, spoil and utterly unclothe thyself of all manner of feeling of thyself, that thou mayest be able to be clothed with the gracious feeling of God Himself'—so he puts it in another closely connected treatise. All this is very like practices traditional in the Russian Orthodox Church and in Buddhism and Hinduism but my immediate point is that the author is most emphatic that his book is not to be read or shown to anyone except to him who has made up his mind 'to be a perfect follower of Christ' – and that as a contemplative monk.

The author of *The Cloud* is quite definite that the way of Mary – that is, a life of contemplation – is better than the way of Martha – that is, active life. The lower part of active life, he says, lies in 'good and honest bodily works of mercy and charity,' and from this a man may go on, while still living an active life, to good spiritual meditations. And thence he may be called to go further to a contemplative life. This fits in with the classical religious training of the Catholic tradition; the threefold way begins with purgation and goes on to illumination and then to union, a path which again would be intelligible to Buddhist or Hindu.

These are deep waters for a layman and I am well aware of my temerity in venturing into them. I have not been through the agony of conversion that Hopkins described:

> The swoon of a heart that the sweep and the hurl of
> thee trod
> Hard down with a horror of height:
> And the midriff astrain with leaning of, laced with fire
> of stress.

Nor have I been weighed down – though perhaps I should – with a burden like Bunyan's. I would not dare to suggest that anyone can reach the spiritual heights described by the saints without purgation – that is to say, self-examination, penitence, and a great deal of hard work. I think incidentally that the beginner who turns to Hinduism or Buddhism – not in a Westernized parlour version but as taught by a genuine believer – will have to tread a similar road there. But the Way of Negation is not for everyone and can come only after some preliminary decisions have been taken – after an assent of the will. And I believe that in the modern world there are many people like Nokes and myself who need help and for whom some steps on the affirmative way may be a preliminary to purgation. Far more emphasis has been placed on beginning with purgation than on the affirmative approach and yet both have always been present in Christianity.

2   THE WAY OF AFFIRMATION

Nokes and I respond to certain passages in the Psalms:

> When I consider thy heavens, the work of thy fingers, the moon and the stars which thou hast ordained – what is man, that thou art mindful of him, and the son of man that thou visitest him?

or again:

> Praise Him with the sound of the trumpet: praise Him with the psaltery and harp: praise Him upon the loud cymbals: praise Him upon the high sounding cymbals. Let everything that hath breath praise the Lord.

Something stirs as we listen to the Benedicite:

> O ye Frost and Cold, bless ye the Lord: O ye Lightnings and Clouds, O ye Whales and all that move in the Waters, O ye Spirits and Souls of the Righteous, bless ye the Lord.

And at the vision of Isaiah:

> And the posts of the door moved at the voice of Him that cried, and the house was filled with smoke.

And again at the vision of Wisdom that seems to foretell John's vision of the Word:[3]

> Doth not Wisdom cry and understanding put forth her voice? I came out of the mouth of the most High and covered the earth as a Cloud. I dwelt in high places and my throne is a cloudy pillar. I was set up from everlasting, from the beginning, or ever the earth was. Before the mountains were settled, before the hills, was I brought forth. When He prepared the heavens, I was there ...

Of course that is Judaism rather than Christianity but it is that sense of praise and wonder – at natural beauty, at the spirit of man and at something more than the spirit of man – that leads me, and I hope is beginning to lead Nokes, to specifically Christian ethics. It is because I see that the wild lily is clothed with beauty which Solomon in all his glory could not match that I understand why the woman of the town who was a sinner was forgiven, why his father killed that calf and made merry for his younger son – who had done so much to deserve instead stern looks and a scolding. A teacher of ethics who was stoic or gnostic or pharisaic or strictly Buddhist would surely have been more pleased with the elder son.

The woman who was forgiven because she loved much has been traditionally identified with Mary Magdalene who in Christian art is usually shown weeping. Indeed, in one of the worst lapses of seventeenth-century affectation, her eyes are called:

> Two walking baths; two weeping motions;
> Portable and compendious oceans.

But it was not because she cried that she was forgiven but because she loved. Her response to life had been positive and this was the point too about the younger son. The contrast between the prodigal son and his elder brother is repeated in the contrast between Mary and Martha; a positive response to life is preferred to the negative. Duty done from a sense of duty is not enough; it leads to a feeling of self-righteousness that turns easily into a grievance – emptiness at the heart instead of positive love. But this brings us back once again to the paradox at the heart of the gospels – for if everyone wasted his substance like the prodigal son, we should be a nation of hired swineherds with no rich father to fall back on. The Protestant ethic of hard work and saving really gets very little support in the gospels – and particularly in Luke.

There is a child's game that everyone knows. Two closed fists are presented to the child; in one there is a sweet or a penny and one is empty. The child has to choose; she cannot have both. And this is, I think, a useful lesson for life in the world of business and politics. You cannot as a rule have both. If it is cheap, it is generally nasty. If you have a big comfortable car, it will use more petrol. But in that country about which the gospels are talking, you can sometimes have both. Jesus himself went into the desert alone to fast and pray and, when he came back he went to supper with rich men, judges and rulers. In the centuries that followed, the Church was confronted again and again with a choice. Had he been God or man? Was God one or three? Was man responsible for his acts or could he do nothing by himself? Was the Creation good or bad? Might images be used as a help to devotion or was that idolatry? And, again and again, the answer, given with a joyous and triumphant smile, was: Both! I come back to these vital decisions in a later chapter; they have been forgotten by the world at large but they really provide the answer to most of our problems today. For the moment what I want to insist on is that Christianity has always found room for the affirmative as well as the negative approach. And—partly for pure pleasure and partly to show how one can lead into the other—let us dwell for a little on two poets.

3   TWO POETS

It has generally been agreed that Traherne is a better poet in prose than in verse. He is uneven and in verse seldom achieves more than a few lines of high quality without spoiling them by what comes next. But it is with what he has to say, not the way he says it, that I am concerned here.[4] He is in love with the world about him. If he goes for a walk it is in order to:

Observe those rich and glorious things
The Rivers, Meadows, Woods and Springs;

We should:

> ... Fly abroad like active Bees
> Among the hedges and the trees
> To cull the dew that lies
> On every Blade,
> From every Blossom till we lade
> Our Minds, as they their Thighs.

His joy in all that the Gnostics despised comes out in his long *Thanksgiving for the Body*, of which the last paragraph contains this:

> I give thee thanks for the beauty of Colours, for the harmony of Sounds, for the pleasantness of Odours, for the sweetness of Meats, for the warmth and softness of our Raiment, and for all my five Senses and all the Pores of my Body, so curiously made ... and for the Preservation of all my Limbs and Senses ...

But limbs and senses are not ends in themselves. Like every physical substance, they are to be used for a spiritual purpose. He listens with delight to the sound of church bells and reflects:

> If Lifeless Earth
> Can make such Mirth
> What then shall Souls above the starry Sphere!
>
> Bells are but Clay that men refine
> And raise from duller Ore
> Yet now as if divine
> They call whole Cities to adore ...
>
> Their iron Tongues
> Do utter Songs
> And shall our stony Hearts make no Reply!

82   DENY YOURSELF

As the bells – once dull metallic ore – are refined until they can perform their special function and utter praises, so must man be refined by rejoicing in the world, which is 'the Temple wherein you are Exalted to Glory and Honour and the visible Porch or Gate of Eternitie … ' Then he will come to realize that the splendour and beauty of common things with which he is 'ravished and intoxicated' are *his*, his own; he will be brought by his joy in them to union with Him 'who is the end of Himself, who doth what He doth that He may be what He is, Wise and Glorious and Bountiful and Blessed in being perfect Love.' But let me quote a slightly longer passage which sums up a great deal of Traherne. He is writing to a lady to whom he was spiritual counsellor.

'As it becometh you to retain a Glorious sense of the World, because the Earth and the Heavens and the Heaven of Heavens are the Magnificent and Glorious Territories of God's Kingdom, so are you to remember always the unsearchable Extent and illimited Greatness of your own Soul; the Length and Breadth and Depth and Height of your own Understanding. Because it is the House of God, a Living Temple and a Glorious Throne of the Blessed Trinity, far more Magnificent and Great than the Heavens, yea, a Person that (is) in Union and Communion with God, is to see Eternity, to fill his Omnipresence, to possess his Greatness, to receive his Gifts, to enjoy the World and to live in his image.'

I shall quote no more, because, splendid though Traherne often is, that does give you the heart of his message. He seems to have made his progress almost entirely by the affirmative way, without purgation. I have only to add that he lived through the Civil War and the Restoration, not exactly settled and peaceful times.

My second poet is Gerard Manley Hopkins. When I

started work on this book, I should have said that he was an example of just what made Nokes uneasy. Hopkins felt that writing poetry was incompatible with his profession as a Jesuit. It was a form of self-indulgence, a kind of luxury. He distrusted as pride the satisfaction he found when his poetry came off, when he had succeeded in expressing exactly his thought and emotion. 'The fine delight that fathers thought' was a pleasure he felt he should put on the bonfire with worldly ambition.

Here we have in one of its harshest forms the challenge to the self which the gospels present. It is harsh because it is subtle. Reason told Hopkins that it was not 'mere self-indulgence' to create something that was beautiful in itself and could be shared with other people. It was hard to get the words right; no one toiled in the workshop more laboriously than Hopkins, lancing his thought with a blowpipe flame, combing and carding it, as he says in various metaphors. And again even the humblest writer knows that what he writes comes in some sense *through* him. It is not his own. And it may bring to others wisdom and growth as well as pleasure. Yet perhaps such arguments were part of the temptation; to Hopkins's sensitive nostril this kind of creativity carried the taint of corruption.

In 1868, when he entered the Society of Jesus, he burnt the verses he had written and 'resolved to write no more, as not belonging to my profession, unless it were by the wish of my superiors. . .' It was not till 1875, and on a 'hint' from his immediate superior at the time, that he broke his silence with that superb symphony *The Wreck of the Deutschland*. All his life, he strove (as W. H. Gardner has pointed out) for an unattainable perfection, whether of language as a poet or of sanctity as a man. But he never lost the feeling that the one search was incompatible with the other. His experience was thus right at the centre of the paradox of impracticable perfection.

What I have only recently come to understand is that his thought and his poetry emphasize the affirmative as well as the negative approach. During the seven years' silence before *The Wreck of the Deutschland*, Hopkins thought he discovered a principle in the philosophy of Duns Scotus that became a constantly recurring note in his poetry. Duns Scotus emphasized the 'thisness' of each individual and it was on this that Hopkins seized. He wrote once of: 'That taste of myself, of *I* and *me*, above and in all things, which is more distinctive than the taste of ale or alum, more distinctive than the smell of walnut-leaf or camphor, and is incommunicable by any means to another man.' There was a similar uniqueness of taste that he recognized everywhere, not only in himself. He called it 'inscape', the quality of 'species or individually distinctive beauty of style' in any object.

With 'inscape' goes another curious word that he did not exactly coin, but used in a special sense of his own, 'sake' or 'sakes'. 'I mean by it', he wrote 'the being a thing has outside itself, as a voice by its echo, a face by its reflection, a body by its shadow, a man by his name, fame or memory, and also that in the thing by virtue of which especially it has this being abroad – and that is something distinctive, marked, specifically or individually speaking, as for a voice and echo clearness: for a reflected image light, brightness ... ' He uses this word, 'sakes' to mean the 'distinctive quality of genius' in Henry Purcell, whose music 'uttered in notes the very make and species of man'. So it is close to 'inscape', which occurs more often. Hopkins wrote during his time as a novice: 'I do not think I have ever seen anything more beautiful than the bluebell I have been looking at. I know the beauty of our Lord by it. Its inscape is mixed of strength and grace ... ' Later, when he had resumed the writing of verse, he wrote: 'As air, melody, is what strikes me most of all in music and design in painting, so design, pattern or what I am in the habit of calling "inscape" is what I above all aim at in poetry.'

Now perhaps 'inscape', the 'thisness' of things, is at the heart of all poetry, in which there is always a counterpoint between sound and meaning, between thought and emotion, between the surface play of actual words and something underlying them which the poet is trying to express. Hopkins gave it a name but the thing itself of course was present in poetry long before Hopkins. John Donne sometimes uses the word 'sphere' in a sense close to Hopkins's use of 'sake' or 'inscape'.[5] There is a special inscape to *Macbeth* as a play, a feeling of darkness and thunder, which is shared by most of the individual lines and images that make up the play. But the 'inscape' of the bluebell or of *Macbeth* has an effect on the beholder and to this too Hopkins gives a special name. It is 'instress'. It illustrates his use of the word as well as his habit of mind that he spoke of the insurrection of Lucifer as 'a dwelling on his own beauty, an instressing of his own inscape ... like a performance on the organ and instrument of his own being ... a sounding, as they say, of his own trumpet ... ' And in this concept of inscape combined with instress, Hopkins comes close to the far less complicated Traherne, who rejoiced in the inscape, the thisness, of everything he saw – rose, cloud or running water – and who felt the instress which broke out in praise and joy. Hopkins is a more accomplished and careful poet, as well as a subtler intellect, but, sometimes, at his simplest, he is saying the same as Traherne:

> I kiss my hand
> To the stars, lovely-asunder
> Starlight, wafting him out of it; and
> Glow, glory in thunder:
> Kiss my hand to the dappled-with-damson west;
> Since, though he is under the world's splendour
> and wonder,
> His mystery must be instressed, stressed;
> For I greet him the days I meet him and bless
> when I understand.

The inscape of the bluebell, lovely in itself, is instressed

by the poet looking at it to become 'the beauty of our Lord'.
This is a sacramental approach to matter and it is at the heart
of all Hopkins's poetry. He sees the falcon in flight and
wonders at 'the achieve of, the mastery of the thing!'
'Brute beauty and valour and act, oh, air, pride, plume here
Buckle!' he cries in ecstasy but goes on at once that the
fire that breaks from Christ is a 'billion Times told lovelier,
more dangerous ... '

Turn where you will in Hopkins, you will find delight
in the thisness of the thing seen. The thing seen is good in
itself because it is, in his thought, an individual act of the
Creator. But the thing seen leads him always to the thing
hidden. One could quote for ever but let me limit myself to
two sonnets.[6] One is 'The Starlight Night':

> Look at the stars! look, look up at the skies!
> O look at all the fire-folk sitting in the air!
> The bright boroughs, the circle-citadels there!
> Down in dim woods the diamond delves! The elves'–
> eyes!
> The grey lawns cold where gold, where quickgold lies!
> Wind-beat whitebeam! Airy abeles set on a flare!
> Flake-doves sent floating forth at a farm-yard scare!

But this beauty in nature is no more than the walls of a barn
that contain wealth within, 'a piece-bright paling' that
reveals through the cracks the glory of brightness inside –
'Christ and his mother and all his hallows'. The point is
made even more explicitly (as Martin Jarrett-Kerr has
pointed out) in the 'Kingfisher' sonnet:

> ... each tucked string tells, each hung bell's
> Bow swung finds tongue to fling out broad its name...
> Selves – goes itself; *myself* it speaks and spells;
> Crying: What I do is me; for that I came.

And that sonnet concludes – in one of those cramped

sestets in which he so often tried to pack too much – that this 'thisness' is the basis of ethics – and of much more than ethics. It is by this same principle of 'going itself' or 'doing its own thing', performing its proper function, that 'the just man justices' and:

'Acts in God's eye what in God's eye he is –
Christ – for Christ plays in ten thousand places,
Lovely in limbs, and lovely in eyes not his
To the Father through the features of men's faces.'

That is to say that the manhood has been taken up into God and that the special function of man – his own proper task like the note of the plucked violin-string or rung bell – is to be taken up into God.

4   NEGATION AND AFFIRMATION

The charge of negativity, which I am sure many people make against Christianity, really includes three separate points. One is physical austerity, which many find pointless and repellent; the second is penitence for sin, of which some are not conscious and on which they feel that Christian language is often exaggerated; the third, which does not arise except for someone who has already made a good deal of progress, is the stripping of the self of all earthly affections – the Way of Negation in its pure form. We can, I think, be clear that physical austerity has not much value in itself, though restraint is part of every system of ethics; the stripping of the self, the true way of negation, will perhaps arise from the start for a few rare spirits, but for most it will be demanded only in part and only after some progress has been made. Penitence is another matter; anyone who wishes to be a Christian must accept that he is not what he would like to be and recognize the need for penitence. Willingly and joyfully we must accept that charge. Yes, there are things we know we should not do, that we try not to do, that we do. There are things we should do and do not. And – yes, that is negative. But it carries with it a positive side. There is always the opposition of Light and Darkness. Penitence will bring you a step closer to what you would like to be. Some may come to self-knowledge, and thus to a knowledge of something more than themselves, in the first place by the way of affirmation, by delight in beauty that is seen or heard. Start by loving the Light rather than hating the Dark. The more vivid the consciousness of beauty – of physical beauty and of all that it stands for – the more conscious man will be of his own smallness and inadequacy. What is man that thou visitest him ... ? And so he may come to penitence.

Hopkins made the step from seen to unseen in almost everything he wrote. He took a sacramental view of matter which he saw as the outward and visible sign of an inward and spirtiual gift. And here I believe is a guide to conduct of the first importance. It means seeing each individual as having a proper function of his own, an inscape, a way of expressing his thisness or doing his thing. If, with all your heart and for its own sake, you do what expresses your thisness – perform your true function, the purpose for which you exist – you have for the moment lost your life in order to find it. If you do it in order to instress your own inscape, as Hopkins put it, or as you and I would say, to blow your own trumpet, you are trying to save your own life only to lose it. It goes without saying that you must try to remember equally the unique thisness of everyone else.

Hopkins had in Robert Bridges a friend who understood his search for perfection in poetry but not in sanctity. A friend who understood both might have suggested to him that in his poetry he did in fact express his thisness as few men have been able to do. That would not have brought him rest; his was not a spirit that could rest. But to me –

and I hope to Nokes – it may be an important step towards understanding the difficulties about which we have been arguing – harnessing, I repeat, the Dove of Inspiration to the Bullock-cart of Normality.

7

Hate Your Father and Mother

I once stayed on the banks of Lake Nyasa with a Bishop who had taken vows of chastity and poverty. He lived in a round hut with a thatched roof and went bare-footed to say Mass in the morning and Compline in the evening. Neither his humility nor his chastity impressed my African companion – interpreter, commentator and driver – who said to me when we left: 'How does the Bishop think he came into the world? And does he not want there to be any more Bishops?'

He put his finger firmly on the central point of this chapter, which is about the fourth aspect of the paradox of perfection. But the traditional Catholic view of the family and of sex is under attack from other angles too. 'If a man come to me and hate not his father and mother and wife and children and brothers, yes, and his own life also, he cannot be my disciple.' A hard saying, indeed, and on top of that there is St Paul's grudging admission that it is better to marry than to burn but better still not to marry. But, as my African friend said, how would the world go on if everyone obeyed those sayings? And does not this distrust of sex – this at best rather churlish admission that it may be necessary but is distinctly to be frowned on – run clean counter to the system of nature? Does it not display again that belief that matter is evil which the Gnostics preached? And once again, we do not live up to what we preach. So long as it professed to be Christian, Western Europe did, officially and corporately, regard chastity with esteem, but in practice prostitution flourished and today the contents of the bookstalls suggest a population of males obsessed with a starved sexuality. Many of the young in Britain and America would say that we – the generation of their parents – by repressing our sexual desires have made them furtive and dirty instead of natural and beautiful.

'Make love not war', say some of the young and others attack the family, as understood in the West, that is, husband, wife and children. It is stuffy, bourgeois and claustrophobic, they say, and the strains and enmities it produces are intolerable. Sometimes, even if there is no legal obstacle to marriage, they prefer to live together without any formal bond, not just as an experiment with the possibility of marriage to come, but because they feel *free* in such a relationship. On the other hand, Africans and Indians alike often criticize the Western family as cold and unloving, far too individualist when compared with the larger family systems of their own quite distinct traditions. Such families, both Indian and African, are three or four generations deep; grandparents and great-grandparents live with their children till death and are taken care of in old age. But in the West we hear of old people whose death is discovered only when the milk-bottles begin to pile up on the doorstep.

The two lines of criticism are opposed; one thinks the family does not give enough freedom to the individual, the other that it gives too much. We live lonely loveless lives in separate boxes and let our parents starve, say the Africans; we force man, wife and child into an artificial box in which they stifle, say the young in the West. They are alike in charging us with a rigid, artificial, joylessness, a gloomy restraint, a withholding of love.

These are broad generalizations; let me make some cautious qualifications. In the country districts of England – and I imagine in most of Europe – where there are still people whose fathers and grandfathers have lived in the same neighbourhood all their lives, the family is still much wider and deeper and the links much closer than the criticism suggests. Grandparents live near their children and look after their children's children; cousins are in close touch and visit each other regularly. The isolated box of husband-wife-children is an urban middle-class development; it has grown up with the move to towns, with more rapid communications and with family dispersal and it has coincided with the decay of religion.[1] So that, even where the charge is true, it is not a consequence of Christian belief, but of economic forces which have proved inimical to Christianity and indeed to other religious systems too.

Nor is either the Indian joint family or the African extended family always the haven of tranquil bliss that is sometimes suggested. There is a scene at which I have never been present but which has been described to me so often that I feel as though I had been there. The young wife, in a family of small landowners in Northern India, has lived perhaps a year in her husband's home, obedient to her mother-in-law, working virtually as a servant. But she wants to go home to her parents, who live in another village often distant two or three days' journey by slow creaking bullock-cart. She asks for leave – using the same word as a soldier uses for leave. But her mother-in-law will not let her go and the voices rise in a crescendo, anger mounting on one side and despair on the other, till the wretched girl springs hysterically to her feet and tries to end her life by jumping into the well. It is a most ineffective way of committing suicide – but it does not suggest a family life in which there is no strain. Indian novels show sister quarrelling with sister, mother with daughter, brother with brother – and though novels, like evidence in a magistrate's court, dramatize moments that are not entirely typical, I have a strong impression that life in a joint family is rich with incident, often of a searing kind. And all I have heard of traditional African life suggests that in the African extended family too, there are disputes and jealousies which demand constant discussion and arbitration and sometimes explode into charges of witchcraft.

I am not convinced then that the small family of two generations is necessarily more productive of tension than the deeper family of three or four generations. There is a wider network of relationships, more choice; a child in trouble with a bad-tempered mother may find a sympathetic aunt or grandmother; he will live in a larger world. But the difference is less than is often suggested and in any case, the smaller family is not specifically Christian, but is rather the product of economic changes which have little to do with religious belief. What Christianity has regarded as peculiarly its own is monogamy; what it has consistently frowned on is sexual intercourse outside marriage. And there can be no question that, in both respects and even in the last ten years, there has been a swing away from traditional Western views. But are the traditional views essentially Christian?

2 LOVE AND LEGAL MARRIAGE

If Christianity has any meaning at all, it is something for all men and it is surely a deep disservice to its central message to link it with customs which may meet the social and economic needs of a particular era and country but are not part of the creed. Christian missionaries in the nineteenth century, particularly in Africa, were often narrowly European in their outlook. They confused what was European with what was Christian. They sometimes regarded it as a triumph to persuade Africans to build square huts instead of round. They frowned on African dancing. I have seen an African in the hottest part of Nigeria wearing a black silk top-hat and a black frock coat, clothes not much less unsuitable than the furs of an Eskimo, imposed by the missionary tradition.

Apart from mere convention, surely today the ideas of 'natural justice' and 'natural law' need to be regarded critically and interpreted with caution. What seems 'natural' in human custom is sometimes no more than what is familiar. I am not saying there are no universal standards of right and wrong. I have not yet heard of a people who would approve of Macbeth's crime – to murder a guest to whom one is bound by loyalty and gratitude. I am saying that it is not always easy to distinguish what is wrong from what is strange. Rules of conduct that are really hygienic have sometimes been given a religious sanction because it was the only sanction available. The Mosaic injunction about pork has been effective far longer than any secular attempts at restricting diet; a Sikh guru's objection to tobacco gets more attention than a government warning on every packet. Rules about sex in particular are usually deeply entwined with emotion; any breach of what is thought natural is regarded with horror. Such rules have often been given a religious sanction, but one people may regard as sacred a rule which for another is reversed. In Jewish traditional law, a man had to marry his brother's widow; in England such a marriage was once prohibited as incest. There is no reason to regard the two-generation family as 'natural'; indeed, for much of that minute section of time of which we have any historical knowledge, the majority of mankind have lived in families three or four generations deep. It is therefore worth considering how far recent changes in ideas about sex are changes of inessential custom and how far they are compatible with Christian belief.

Of course there have always been breaches of rule. The young have sipped; their elders have strayed. Plenty of men have had mistresses – but usually because there was an obstacle to marriage or because the woman was regarded by the convention of the day as unsuited for the social duties that would go with the marriage. There has usually been at least a genuflexion towards permanence and – almost as often – an inner desire for it. In a mood of youthful cynicism and flippancy, John Donne could write:[2]

> I can love her and her and you and you,
> I can love any so she be not true –

but he was surely always in search of a deep and permanent love and eventually found it. Pepys might be an amorous middle-aged trifler with serving wenches but he took the institution of marriage for granted and had no intention of upsetting his own. Beatrice and Benedick, Millamant and Mirabell, are both high-spirited couples jealous of their personal independence; they fence, each eager to make it seem that it is the other who is submitting – but they never question the nature of the bond into which they are being drawn. But it is different today.

It has quite recently become a custom for a man and a woman to live together without concealment in a union which continues from year to year, but with no legal bond. There may be or may not be an intention of permanence. There are, by definition, no rules in this kind of relationship and it would be rash to generalize as though there were, but the couples I have met say emphatically that they are not promiscuous and that it is a 'caring' relationship. They say also that it is not mainly a matter of money. Still, it can hardly be doubted that it would not be so common if the woman had not usually a job or a career that made her independent financially. Calculations about income-tax may affect it and the traces that remain of legal inequality in marriage. I have heard of a case in which a man will not marry because, if he did, part of his new wife's earnings would go in alimony to a former wife. Careers may clash and one partner may want to take a post in, say, the United States which would mean the other either giving up a career or breaking up the union. If that is part of the reason for not accepting a legal tie, it means of course that career comes first and the relationship comes second and is thought of as less permanent.

There are other factors too, of which the ability to control childbirth is one. In most cases, a couple living in this way have decided not to have children. But that too asks for explanation, because for thousands of years people *have* wanted children. Here too it is not enough to say that economic considerations alone have brought about the change. In financial terms, the cost of bringing up children is less for the middle classes than it was two generations ago; they are less likely to feel that private education is necessary, though the cost in time and effort for themselves is greater because they no longer have servants. The custom so far is mainly middle class though it seems likely to spread. One thing in common in the two decisions, to have no children and to live together without legal ties, is a changed attitude to permanence and the future.

Until quite lately, man has usually felt himself to be one rung on a ladder in time. The feeling was strong in most of the traditional African societies; the living came between the dead ancestors and the unborn descendants and had responsibilities to both. Some such feeling has been traditional in Chinese and Indian civilizations; it was a part of Greek and Roman religion. In modern Europe it has been attached to land, not only in the great landowning families but among people like my own grandfather, who farmed the land his father and grandfather had farmed and lived in the house they had lived in. As you went up the stairs in that house you saw the sampler that Great Aunt Emma had worked in 1842. It gave you a feeling of being something small against a permanent background. And that feeling was present among those whose families had lived in the same group of villages for generations and were buried in the same churchyard. For all such people, time has extended backwards and forwards with little expectation of change.

That sense of permanence has gone. Man in the modern city has become a point in space and a point in time instead of part of a continuity in both. Change is so rapid that young people hardly bother to consider their old age. Things will be so different then, they say, that it is idle to make plans. The state will look after either of us who survives; if the survivor is too old to work there will be a pension. This is not a world, some of them say, into which a really responsible person would want to bring children.

And as for ourselves, if we *can* stick together, the understanding and tenderness that grow from fitting in with
each other's ways will have been established by the time
we are old, just as surely as if there had been a legal bond.
The law, they say, is irrelevant; what would it add? A piece
of paper means nothing. If we *were* married and wanted to
part, it would be right to part. So let us not make complica-
tions by bringing in lawyers.

Far too many conventional marriages, they will add, go
on far too long; they linger on when all tenderness has
ceased and the strain of bearing with each other and of
keeping up appearances smothers for both partners all life
and spontaneity, not only in relation to each other but to
other people as well. They put on masks – cold and grey or
bright and shiny – but lifeless. But for us keeping together
is a challenge. It is stimulating and invigorating. We are
freed from the extra strain of putting up with each other's
relations. Our friends on the whole are people who feel as
we do about freedom. Our relationship is a matter of delic-
acy and continual experiment. Nothing can be taken for
granted. There can be no room for the selfishness or even
brutality that may grow up in legal marriage; the other
party would leave at once.

This is common to all the couples I have talked to.
But there is a difference between the pioneers who led the
way and the younger generation. Some of the pioneers
begin to be conscious of a faint guilt at settling down so
respectably in a relationship almost indistinguishable from
the institution at which they were once determined to
protest. But the younger generation take it for granted;
to some of them it is legal marriage that is abnormal.

Here let me abandon without a fight some ground to my
imaginary opponent, whom we agreed to call Nokes. The
feeling of continuity between ancestors and descendants is
clearly not peculiarly Christian; it has been stronger in
China, India, and traditional Africa than in Christendom.
And while I am conscious of a slight feeling of outrage that

a man should feel he need not make provision for his wife after his death, that feeling has not much to do with Christianity; it involves a different way of looking at the state and personal effort and a different economic relationship between man and woman, but it need not mean that he does not feel responsible for her well-being. And I will agree at once that Nokes has a valid point if he says that the kind of union we have been discussing may well be more humane and loving than many legal marriages. I agree that legality is not the specifically Christian aspect of marriage. The legal position of a married woman in Victorian England was unjust and therefore un-Christian; her property was legally her husband's and she herself came near to being his property. The law was not in accordance with the Christian concept of marriage, which is a mutual promise to love, to honour, to cherish and to share. Of course, in spite of a legal system which fell far short of justice, hundreds of thousands of couples did live together within that system in love and happiness. But the contract might be entered into to round off an estate or to save an impoverished family, and without any true respect between the persons; indeed such a possibility was as much the backbone of the Victorian novel as of the Restoration comedy. I will agree with Nokes that the union without a legal bond which I have just been talking about may well be much nearer a true Christian marriage than a loveless match for money, or a marriage in which the parties have really no intention of giving up anything for each other.

Here I am at once beset by difficulties from all angles. Nokes – a romantic at heart – will say triumphantly that the essence of love is freedom. How can you enter into a contract to love? It is like a publisher's contract, which is not a true contract at all, only a declaration of intention, because no one can be forced to write a book. All you can do is to make an agreement as to certain arrangements that will follow if the intention is carried out. And a Roman friend who is a rigorist may say severely that there can be no 'more or less' about Christian marriage; it is a *sacrament,* which is either valid or not valid and it is permanent. My African friend will say that he simply does not understand the idea of a marriage which does not hope for children. And I can only hope to meet these difficulties by starting again in a more positive and constructive sense.

3 A MORE CONSTRUCTIVE APPROACH

Let us go back to the beginning. I suggested that in four respects – property, violence, self-assertion, sex – Christianity was open to attack as preaching a perfection which in practice Christendom – the traditional Christian society of Europe – has ignored and which, if it had ever been seriously followed, would have destroyed organized society. Here I think a distinction should be made. The attack on property is strong in the gospels, much weaker in the later history of the Church; much the same is true of violence. But in respect of sex the emphasis has been reversed. The grudging attitude to sex is hardly there in the gospels; it develops later. When Jesus spoke of 'hating father and mother', he was not condemning the family but saying that family ties must not be allowed to stand in the way of a man's doing his essential task in life. He may have to leave his family and follow his star, exercise his special thisness, praise God by creation; nothing must stand in his way. As to sexuality Jesus had much less to say. He forgave two women whom men condemned; tradition suggests that one of them became his follower. He said that marriage was till death. He said that there would be no sexuality after death, but few will question that. The idea that sexuality is shameful in itself is not to be found in his teaching, but his followers thought they must anticipate Heaven and behave as though they were there already.

Now it is an essential part of my argument that Christianity gives Light – a vision of Light – but leaves freedom to men, struggling in the world, to find exact interpretations.

They are frightened of freedom; they run away from its responsibilities. They make rigid rules but these need continuous modification. It is a Christian dogma that the Church – that is, the followers of Christ in action – have been guided by the Holy Spirit and I believe this to be true. But the Spirit does not dictate; it guides, it leads. Men have often misinterpreted its guidance. They have often ignored it. They have that freedom. It is still leading and guiding and the definitions and conclusions of one age have to be continually restated in new language and with a new emphasis for changing conditions. And this area of sex and the family is one in which new thought is needed.

In its early decisions on the basic points of Christianity the struggling Church again and again reached conclusions that were joyous and affirmative. They refuted heresies that were limited and essentially negative. But a heresy always states part of the truth and the conclusions – which state a wider truth – have usually been steeped in paradox. They have to because the truth itself is many-sided but in addition the conclusions have to make provision for saints but must also be of help to ordinary folk, who know they will never be perfect but who can be helped to be better than they would otherwise be. The Church decided that it was impossible to banish sex from the world altogether – as some had thought they could when they expected the second coming and the end of the world at any moment. The attempt had been a mistake; it was Gnostic and implied that the creation was evil. Man had been told to be fruitful and multiply. Yet some balance was needed – and it is hard to be balanced about sex, which comes so close to the centre of man's being. It is hard for the young to be balanced about desires that cause such pain and such pleasure and which are so intimately linked with self-esteem and self-realization. It is not much easier for those who are older; attitudes taken up in youth get rigid and become sacred. Restraint may have been enforced in youth by social convention and lack of op-

56760

portunity – which in their turn arose in part from women's economic dependence and from the inability to control childbirth. When senility has reduced the chances of abandoning it, restraint may come to be regarded as a virtue, to be jealously enforced on the young. What is socially desirable and what makes for holiness have been inextricably confused. It is hard indeed for anyone to look at sex with any degree of detachment.

But circumstances have changed. Women are often financially independent. They can control childbirth. The *social* need for the extreme strictness of rigid rule has passed; the need remains for some guidance as to what, from the quite different point of view of *holiness*, is better or worse. The need for companionship, whether with or without physical expression in sex, has grown greater in modern life because of the break-up of local ties and relationships of blood. I suggest, therefore, a new approach that is not a matter of: 'This is right and that is wrong', but rather a matter of degree, something which can be expressed in religious terms and marked on a kind of scale like a thermometer, at one end being the more sacramental approach and at the other the more idolatrous. Religious terms are needed, because sex comes so near to the centre of man's being that he will not be whole unless his view of sex is related to his view of the world. And that will make sense only if it brings man's behaviour and hopes into focus with pain and birth, death and eternity – that is to say, if it is a religious view. Every human culture of which I have heard has made some attempt to bring sex into such a focus and has usually tried to dramatize its conclusions by ritual. Ritual and sacrament in religion, symbols in poetry and drama, resemble each other in that within a wide meaning apparent to all, there is room for a varied range of personal interpretation. What I suggest is that it is on this scale between sacrament and idolatry that the essence of the Christian conclusion lies.

At the end of the last chapter, I was discussing the nega-

tive and affirmative ways and I quoted Hopkins as an instance of an affirmative approach to religion by way of the
beauty of natural objects and of the self-hood, the thisness,
of each individual object. I used the word 'sacramental' to
describe this approach. St Augustine defined a sacrament as
the visible sign of an invisible reality. This is wider than
ecclesiastical use today but it expresses exactly what I find
in Hopkins. For him each physical object is the visible sign
of its own invisible reality and it invariably leads him to
thoughts of what was for him a far wider and deeper reality.
By idolatrous I mean an entirely contrary attitude to objects
of sense and physical acts, an attitude which treats them as
having no inner meaning of their own. They may become
idols to be served or things to be collected for their own
sakes. And it is a kind of reversed idolatry to treat objects –
still more animals, still more people – as though they had no
special qualities of their own, no thisness, no meaning. It
is to behave as though they had meaning only in so far as
they minister to my needs. It is self-idolatry. Stamp-
collecting may perhaps be a harmless kind of idolatry and
keeping battery hens is reversed idolatry.

Thus a sexual act which expresses affection and companionship as well as physical attraction would be nearer the
sacramental end of the scale than one in which there was
no concern for each other as persons, perhaps only a sense
of physical need and the payment of money. That lies far
out at the idolatrous end and so of course does the behaviour
of the collector of amorous scalps. He is feeding his own
self-idolatry. Once that distinction is made, it seems to
follow that the invisible reality expressed is very much more
real – that is, more intense – and the relationship in my
language more sacramental, if the commitment to each
other is permanent. In that case, it costs something. It
means accepting responsibility for each other, sharing not
only worldly goods but sickness and health, anxiety and
hope, success and adversity. If the couple mean to keep
together, they will plan together an alteration to the house,

they will save up for a holiday, consult whether they can afford a gramophone record or a picture. Every shared activity, every act of courtesy and consideration, every task divided, every bed made, every cup of tea, every trifling thing fetched to save the other trouble, build up in the end, sacramentally, to represent the relationship which begins to exist between them and which they mean shall grow. They accept – whether with active pleasure or with humorous resignation – responsibility for each other's cousins and aunts. I should like that permanence, that responsibility, that intention of courtesy and consideration, to be expressed ritually. Ritual of course does imply the approval of a like-minded community. Legality in the eyes of the state is less important. But it is the binding nature of the relationship in the eyes of the two parties that really counts. The cups of tea matter more than the ring.

The conventional marriage which the unconventional couple referred to just now as having 'gone on far too long' had ceased to be sacramental, gone dead, failed to grow into the kind of tender consideration for each other that should develop with age. But the use of the phrase 'gone on too long' is revealing. It is the language of the affair; it assumes impermanence at the heart of the relationship, as opposed to exchange and sharing.

The question to ask, then, is not whether a relationship involving sex is legal but whether it is sacramental in the sense I have suggested. A legal marriage in which there is no companionship, no sharing of tastes, no tenderness, is far indeed from being sacramental. In the end, the question is what the two persons are prepared to do for each other. And this involves more than momentary ecstasy, more than obsession with exciting revelations of character, tricks of speech, movements and gestures, more than the joy of finding feelings reciprocated, more than delight at being in each other's company, more than what is generally called being in love. For that – most of us know sadly enough – will for most of us pass unless it is expressed in a permanent commitment, an act of faith. It has to be turned into shared activity. It needs an outward and visible sign.

> For, nor in nothing, nor in things
> Extreme, and scatt'ring bright, can love inhere ...

This, the translation of ephemeral vision into enduring habit, is just what I mean by harnessing the dove of inspiration to the bullock-cart of normality.

8

Third Interlude: Joyful Truth

I THE HERESY THAT MATTER IS EVIL

Let me in this third interlude make good what I have said more than once, that the big decisions of the early Church were essentially affirmative and took account of human weakness. I am thinking of the great heresies which recur throughout the history of Christendom, changing their names and reviving under new forms, taking new shapes in new regions, absorbing features from each other and from systems of belief outside Christendom. They are still alive today and influence countless men and women who have never heard their names. To recognize and repudiate them is a step towards the positive affirmative faith that Nokes and I are looking for.

Let us look first in a little more detail at the group of heresies of which the essence was the belief that matter was evil. If Christendom has sometimes done less than justice to the glories and shames of the body, that is perhaps by the infection of these heresies. There were the various Gnostic sects at the beginning of the Christian era and later the followers of Mani, who were called Manichaean, a Zoroastrian heresy as much as a Christian.[1] There were many later forms – Paulicians, Messalians, Bogomils, Patarenes, Cathari and Albigensians and variants to all of these. These sects often gave absurd and confused accounts of the Creation, in some of which the Jehovah of the Old Testament, stern and revengeful, became a villain, hostile to the prime cause, sometimes a brother or colleague of Satan. Those who opposed Jehovah thus became heroes and a cult of the

Serpent arose because he had scored off Jehovah in the Garden of Eden.

That was a by-way. In the direct line, since the created world must be rejected, extreme austerity was to be admired and all earthly pleasure to be deplored, particularly marriage and the generation of children. Escape from matter was the one good and this could only be achieved by the highest order of mankind – the finally initiated, the Perfecti, the Illuminati, the Pneumatikoi or Spiritual, as they were called in different sects and at different periods. Sometimes this highest grade of being lived only on Light, as some orchids do; by a convenient arrangement, however, anything they swallowed turned into Light. I have been told that His late Highness, the Aga Khan, was similarly able to turn champagne into milk. In the last period in Languedoc before their extermination, it was common among the Manichaeans to end their lives by fasting. There was a rite, the *Consolamentum*, which combined the purposes of Baptism, Confirmation, Communion and Supreme Unction and, once that had been accepted, any sin that might follow would be beyond forgiveness and it was logical to embark on the *Endura* or sanctified suicide by starvation. Thus the Perfecti could escape for ever from matter and the cycle of Re-birth.

There were usually two lower grades below the Perfecti, the lowest being called the Material or the Earthy, men with no spark of the divine. They would be born again, which would further the devil's work and prolong the existence of matter. Matter could only be ended if all men became Perfecti and escaped from matter. To die in a lower grade was thus bad but it was even worse to produce children. Casual debauchery was therefore often regarded as less culpable than marriage and sodomy preferable to intercourse that might lead to procreation. It was this belief and the prevalence of the heresy in Bulgaria that enriched the French and English languages with a term of abuse whose acerbity the years have softened. At various stages of their history, there were Manichaean groups who advocated nudism, or that all males should be castrated, or that it was a duty to sin in order to make forgiveness possible. A belief that seems to have recurred at various stages was that Jesus entered the body of his mother by her ear and left by the same route. Often the idea that all matter was evil led to the other ancient heresy that Jesus had only *seemed* to be a man.

It would be wrong to linger on the absurdities to which this one belief sometimes led. St Augustine was for many years a Manichee and a system that could hold that powerful mind cannot have been absurd in itself. But he became gradually convinced that it was not intellectually or spiritually defensible; no wide-spreading system of theology was ever established for the Manichees. Their one basic idea gained ground because of its simplicity wherever peasants were oppressed; they understood a world that was hostile and painful. A simple mind, pondering on that one and apparently self-evident fact, with no instruction and no theology, might easily be led into absurdity. And of course it was more likely to spread where the clergy were corrupt and, once it had a footing, it was made use of by nobles who wanted to lay hands on the possessions of the Church or by rulers who wanted to assert their sovereignty against feudal overlords. It spread through the Balkans, where princes, dukes and barons found admirable opportunities for self-aggrandizement in the rivalry of the Eastern and Western churches. It made odd little pockets with strange local variations of belief; it would be strong here and then it would be suppressed and then it would bubble up again somewhere else. From Bulgaria the heresy spread to Bosnia and then across the Adriatic to Lombardy and over the Alps to France. Crushed to the East of the Rhône, it grew stronger in Languedoc and spread to Gascony.

In Southern France all the ingredients for its success were present; a corrupt and careless clergy, an unhappy peasantry, nobles anxious to grab church lands and establish their

power both against each other and against the Count of
Toulouse, who in his turn hoped for independence from
the King of France. National sovereignty was still fluid.
Society was in a state to which could be applied the Indian
proverb: 'The man with the stick gets the buffalo.' The
peasants listened to heretic missionaries who cared for
them, who preached a message they could understand,
and who lived a life much purer than the Catholic clergy.
The lords saw their chance and made use of the peasants.
And some nobler spirits, especially among the women,
were genuinely converted to lives of voluntary poverty and
care for others. Yet the essential message of the Albigensian
creed was suicidal; to bring a child into the world or to
make any lasting improvement in man's condition was to
do the devil's work.

Mission after mission was sent to preach the Catholic
faith. The Dominican Order began its work here. But in
face of the appalling corruption of the local clergy, the
missions failed. At the beginning of the thirteenth century,
from the Rhône to Gascony almost the whole countryside
seemed lost for ever; the heresy was openly preached;
peasants, cities, nobles alike rejected the doctrines of the
Trinity, the Incarnation, the Resurrection and the Atonement and repudiated marriage, the bearing of children and
ultimately life itself. At last, reluctantly and under strict
conditions which his agents disregarded – and meant from
the start to disregard – Innocent III gave his assent to the
Crusade against the South and the slaughter of the Albigenses began. If there had been unworthy motives among the
Southern heretics, the rapacity of the Crusaders – most
of them barons from the North in search of new estates –
was even more shameless, and to avarice they added a callous
brutality. It is a tale of tragedy in the deepest sense, the
tragic waste of noble aims on either side, lost in a welter of
folly, greed and cruelty.

That heresy in Languedoc was an extreme expression of
the dualism between light and darkness that is at the heart

of St John's Gospel. The Catholic view was that both good and evil were present in the world and were in conflict but that the Creation was good; the manhood had been taken up into God and eventually the conflict would be reconciled. The Manichaean was that the conflict was absolute and could not be reconciled, matter was evil and the spirit could escape from it only by utter separation. Today, in the materialist affluent societies of the West, the tendency among the majority, particularly among the old and respectable, is rather to take material things as ends in themselves. But there are people in revolt against this materialist, idolatrous attitude, and among them are many of the young. They often fly to the other extreme. They do not want *organized* religion; they think that organization must banish inspiration. They make a sharp contrast between the illumination of the spirit and the dull, earthy, material details of buildings, lighting and heating, training and teaching. They want something pure and holy and divorced from matter. And this leads to queer sects and queer new theologies.

This is surely to be expected. If you reject the accumulated wisdom of the past, the trial and error of centuries, it is likely that oddities will appear. Human knowledge only began to make strides when writing was invented and it became possible to store up skill and information. Before that, a man could only draw on what his father taught him and what he heard from the tiny circle of people he knew. Writing immensely widened the material with which he could build. It is surely arrogant to reject all that accumulated wisdom and rely on the individual's unaided intelligence. If, on the other hand, it is the direct inspiration of the Holy Spirit that is claimed, surely it is wise to reflect that others too may have been inspired; further, it is always the nature of such inspiration to leave undiminished the freedom that is an essential part of the Christian revelation. Man is not a tape-recorder; he has a duty to interpret, consider and arrange in the light of the past.

Again and again, in the course of two thousand years, movements have come into being whose leaders have been repelled by matter and fearful of idolatry but who, instead of bringing matter and spirit together into a wise sacramentalism, have tried to start again from the beginning, ignoring the experiments of the early Christians and the conclusions of the great Councils. In consequence, they have put burdens on the human spirit too great to bear. This is what Ronald Knox called Enthusiasm. Among these sects are the Montanists, the Donatists, the Waldensians, the Puritans of the Commonwealth in England, Ranters and Shakers, Pentecostalists and Fifth Monarchy Men – all of whom have based their beliefs on a distaste for the created world that is essentially Manichaean. So today among the young have been Flower People and Jesus Folk. And there have been others too within the formal boundaries of the Church, movements such as Jansenism, and those Franciscan zealots who were judged to have gone beyond the extreme limits permitted. They went to their deaths rapt in the belief that they alone had the truth. Manichaeism is an error of noble minds and more to be respected than idolatry.

Thinking about this puritan heresy has led me to picture a scale between a Manichaean rejection of matter and an idolatrous over-estimate of its importance. And when considering sex we pictured a scale between sacramentalism and idolatry. The two scales are really one, because sacramentalism provides a sane, human and workable alternative to the Manichaean extreme as well as to the idolatrous. Let us illustrate this scale, by looking at two concepts of a Christian community, the parish and the 'gathered community'.

The 'gathered community' is of course the older; by definition, the first Christians were all converts and had to be gathered if they were to have any corporate life. But after the decision of Constantine, when, in Charles Williams's phrase, all hypocrisy became Christian, when, gradually and step by step, whole areas became nominally Christian, the parish took its place. In the parish, it was taken for granted that everyone in varying degrees accepted the Faith. It followed that children should be baptized as soon as possible after birth; they should grow up within the community as members, within the blessing and protection of the sacramental order. I am giving a quasi-sociological reason for a practice which was discussed in very different terms and justified theologically by very different arguments – but the fact that two lines of argument reach the same conclusion does not invalidate either. The practice of infant baptism was enforced by the sanction that the souls of the unbaptized would be condemned for eternity to limbo – a doctrine that has been variously interpreted and on which I must not digress. The point about the parish system which arises from infant baptism is that everyone in the parish shares, in some degree, in its sacramental life. Even if the priest is unworthy, the rites he celebrates are valid; even those who do not attend corporate worship in church are taken up in the prayers of those who do. So long as the whole system is not openly repudiated by witchcraft or heresy, the idlest, the most careless, the most ignorant man in the parish has some part in its life and there is the possibility that the Holy Spirit may begin to reach him.

This ties up with a modern problem that arose also in St Paul's time. As it was presented to him, a couple had been married before the Christian dispensation began, perhaps by Jewish rites, perhaps by some pagan custom. One, but not the other, is converted to the new Faith. Let us suppose it is the wife. What is she to do? Let her not leave him, says Paul; the unbelieving husband is sanctified by the wife and the children will be holy. There is the answer for the modern couple too and also by implication the true doctrine of the parish.

That is the one ideal, based on the concepts of sacramentalism, of sharing and of recognizing human weakness. It carries with it the danger of trying to include the indifferent. But where the gathered community has revived and has taken the place of the parish, where the conscious choice of an adult is necessary for baptism, there is a contrary – and I believe a more serious – danger of excluding all but enthusiasts. I have read of communities in New England where a young man was required at the age of eighteen or nineteen to make a public proclamation of his faith. He had to undergo conversion and announce before the congregation that he was saved. The alternative was something near excommunication; this must have put an intolerable strain on any sensitive young man, excluded honest doubters and also excluded men of extrovert character and strong sensuality who, if not forced to so radical a choice so early, might have grown in time into a more moderate belief. This insistence on conversion revives the old Manichaean division between the perfect or initiated and the mass of the common people. It forgets that very early decision of the Church that nothing should be called common or unclean and that the Gentiles should be welcomed as believers. It forgets something admirably expressed by Chesterton:[2] 'When Christ at a symbolic moment was establishing his great society, he chose for its corner-stone neither the brilliant Paul nor the mystic John but a shuffler, a snob, a coward – in a word, a man.'

All this suggests that if the Catholic is sometimes in danger of idolatry, the Protestant must be as careful to avoid Manichaeism.

2 THE HERESY THAT MAN IS SELF-SUFFICIENT

By far the most prevalent today of the perennial heresies is the Pelagian. It occurs in various forms. Pelagius himself is believed to have been Irish, or possibly Scottish, a monk who came to Rome when past his youth about the year 400. He and his pupils taught that man falls into sin only by temptation and bad example – as the result of what would now be called environment; there is no such thing as original sin inherent in man. One of his close disciples, Coelestius, was arraigned for heresy and the doctrine came to the notice of St Augustine, who attacked it over a period of many years in no less than fifteen treatises. The controversy was couched in terms which today most of us would find quite unconvincing. Nonetheless, Augustine was right and Pelagius was wrong. To say that the sin of Adam became a hereditary taint in his descendants is to me in one sense a myth that I regard as quite untrue, but it is inspired truth if you look on it as a metaphorical statement of an evolutionary and psychological fact. Sin is a technical term for animal self-assertion, strong in infants and controlled in well-integrated adults by their recognition of their obligation to others. It is innate in the child from birth if not before. You can hear it in that first angry squall of outrage at being expelled from a warm, dark, comfortable Garden of Eden to a cold challenging world that demands constant adaptation to the ways of others. It was planted there during the evolutionary process and without it man would not have survived as a species.

Pelagius might have checked this by observation if he had been able to watch the behaviour of his grandchildren in a permissive age. He never had the pleasure of seeing their natural selfishness, greed, aggression and self-assertion gradually give way to the gentle guidance of loving parents. He had no grandchildren after the flesh, poor man, and thought children were naturally good – and would stay good if not interfered with by evil influences. But he was the spiritual grandfather of an immense progeny, including Jean-Jacques Rousseau, who thought that man had been noble when he lived in a state of primitive savagery and would return to a pure and virtuous simplicity if he could only rid himself of the corrupting influence of priests and kings. 'Man is born free and is everywhere in chains … ' he began his famous treatise. What rubbish! Man is born the slave of physical needs which can only be satisfied by other people and it is only at rare periods in history that – by the grace of God and as a result of constant effort on his own part and a high degree of organization and co-operation with others— he has ever achieved any degree of freedom to control his destiny and realize the full possibilities that lie within him. Marx too was a Pelagian when he preached that the state would wither away in a golden age when Capitalism had been ended. And at the beginning of this century Shaw and Wells frequently preached a Pelagian optimism; man by his own efforts would reach various Utopias by changes in the system of government or by the distribution of wealth.

But by now we have learnt that affluence is as corrupting as poverty. Selfishness and greed do not get less when people have enough to eat; they grow with the expectation of plenty. And in a society without faith, selfishness and greed will continue to grow. The Christian belief, on the other hand, is that bondage to such forms of idolatry can only be ended by accepting partnership in the task of trying to establish the City of God. This means a realistic recognition of man's imperfection; he can do nothing by himself and he needs at every turn the guidance of the Holy Spirit, which he is more likely to find when operating within a community and which he will need to interpret in the light of human experience.

3   THE HERESY THAT GOD IS REMOTE

There are two other great heresies of the past alive today. The Arians insisted so jealously on the unity and remoteness of God that they would not allow that the manhood had been taken up into God or that God works in and through man. And this surely makes their God so cold and distant that human joy and human suffering alike become meaningless. The God in whom most agnostics do not believe is an Arian God and not the God of the Incarnation. It takes the meaning from human life if you do not believe, consciously or unconsciously, in the God of the Incarnation:

Warm-laid grave of a womb-life grey;
  Manger, maiden's knee;
The dense and the driven Passion, and frightful sweat...

Nonetheless, there are many modern Arians. What they believe has the great advantage that it is simpler and easier to explain than Christian belief. As I said before, Christians, confronted with the question of whether Jesus was God or Man, replied: 'Both!' They further added that something had happened to man; the manhood had been taken up into God, or, to translate that phrase – as near as one can, for it will not translate exactly – into prosaic language, it had become possible for man, here on earth and in time, to grow beyond the evolutionary heritage of animal self-hood and realize something of the divine possibility that lies within him.

That Jesus was the Son of God and had taken up the Manhood into God is not the kind of statement that can be put into the language of Euclidean thought.[3] It is not a proposition of the same order as that the three angles of a triangle make two right-angles. If you are asked in a magistrate's court whether you took an apple from an old woman's basket, that is a question to which you can answer yes or no. To give a simple answer to the question: 'Are you the Son of God?' was quite another matter. The question did not mean the same to the Court and to the Prisoner. To answer yes would have been as misleading as to answer no. The Jews expected a saviour, but they expected him to come with the clouds of heaven as a supernatural manifestation. That expected saviour is called the Son of Man in the Book of Daniel and Jesus took that phrase and used it of himself. He used it habitually but made special use of it in the inquiry before the High Priest. The phrase in itself implies, simply by those three words taken literally, that he saw himself as the representative Man, but he clearly meant also to identify himself with the promised Saviour. The secret, the discovery which he alone saw, which even his disciples would not believe until he was dead, was that the Saviour was not to come with the clouds of heaven, but in pain and poverty. This was the revelation or decision or discovery—it is all three—made in the desert when Ivan's wise and dread spirit tempted him.

But the modern Arian does not understand this. Humanist and rationalist though he is, at the back of his mind is a feeling that the Son of God would have come in a chariot of fire. He would have floated down from the Temple; he would have come down from the Cross. Since he did none of these things, and since to people of this habit of mind any question must be such that it can be answered yes or no, then he was man and man only; any saying that suggests he was not is an accretion, something added by his followers after his death. Indeed, I have recently seen it asserted that only four of his sayings are to be regarded as undoubtedly his—and that because they contradict the claim to divinity and must therefore have escaped the vigilance of editors.[4]

This is to base the interpretation of the evidence on the dogma that he made no such claim—a dogma which in its turn proceeds from accepting the Arian hypothesis. In my view, on the other hand, it is fantastic to imagine an editor or editors of such genius as to invent the great mass of teachings and sayings—all the sayings but those four!— through which runs the note of thisness, of a single personality, a personality who spoke with authority and power, knowing that he was the promised saviour, carrying with him the calm conviction that arose from that great discovery made in the desert, that the Son of Man would not swagger about in a halo but would on the contrary have nowhere to lay his head. We both make an act of faith— the modern Arian and I. Mine is that the evidence we have is based on a strong verbal tradition of the sayings of a unique personality who was both human and divine; the Arian distrusts all these sayings unless they run counter to what has been generally believed by Christians and unless they support his own dogma that the human and the divine are utterly separate and that Jesus was 'not divine'.

It was not only his followers who thought he meant to establish a body of believers in a new Message, or, as we should say, to found a Church. So did the orthodox Jews of that period, who therefore repudiated him. If he did habitually use that phrase 'The Son of Man', he meant to establish that body. Surely no Jew could hear it without thinking of the prophecy in the Book of Daniel in which it is used of the coming Messiah? And in that case, the idea that he was 'just a good man' has to be abandoned; you must either accept the claim or go the whole hog and charge him with delusions of grandeur. If he did not use that phrase, who – I should like to know – was the remarkable genius who attributed the phrase to him, who invented so many of his sayings and invested his personality with the power that has impressed so many millions? And why was that anonymous genius so anxious to bolster up into a church an oppressed and persecuted sect against whom every man's hand was turned? How much easier life would have been for Peter and James and John – and for that unknown genius – if they had gone quietly home and forgotten the whole episode!

The modern Arian is to be found in many forms and, because his God, if he has a God at all, is remote from matter and flesh and human-kind, he is almost bound to be also either a kind of Manichee or a kind of Pelagian. He is bound to think either that God is too remote to be responsible for the world or that man is self-sufficient.

The fourth great heresy is also a branch of the Manichean. The original Docetists could not believe that the sufferings of Christ were real, as are the sufferings of men. They taught that it was merely an apparition, a kind of phantom, that took his place and seemed to suffer. There are not now so many people in England as there were before the First World War who persuade themselves that suffering is not real. But though they see it on television, there are still Docetists who say in their heart: 'It will not touch me.' It is one of the dangers of affluence to close the eyes to suffering, to deny that blood and pain and death are part of life and that, in this suffering, God and man are mysteriously made one. Today that is the essence of the Docetic heresy, which has so often accompanied the denial of the flesh and of the Incarnation. It is against that complacent escapism and against the awful remoteness of an unincarnate God who exists alone, for himself and in himself, that John triumphantly proclaimed the Incarnation. The Word became flesh and dwelt among us.

It is in the light of that truth that we must find a way of approaching all the questions I have been asking, about property and violence, about the self and sex and the family. It is here that we come to what I hope is the constructive stage of this book.

9

Do This

In the earlier chapters of this book, I was mainly asking questions, sometimes through the mouth of an imaginary adversary, whom I called Nokes. But I was also, particularly in the interludes, moving in a rather crab-like way towards the synthesis which I must in the end attempt. There are still some positive points to establish – principles, ways of looking at things – and the first of these is my use of the word 'sacramental'. It is a metaphor central to what I see as a Christian approach to life and I must explain it more clearly.

I spoke of a sacramental act, in a broader sense than the ecclesiastical. In that narrower sense it means an act directly connected with the special sacraments hallowed by long tradition and by the Church's use. I have used the term more widely, meaning an act that fitted St Augustine's phrase about the visible sign of an invisible truth. Let me add something to that. It must not merely stand for something more than itself, an invisible truth, but also in some degree it must be set aside as representative of that truth. What the act represents may be an emotional experience, an intellectual insight, a personal relationship; it may be steadfast belief or constantly renewed intention; but it is, or is part of, something ongoing, something continuous, something too big to be always in the forefront of consciousness. In a true sacrament in the ecclesiastical sense, the act is consciously set aside as representative of the truth; in my wider metaphorical sense there may be no conscious dedication of the representative moment.

To illustrate what I mean, let us think a little of eating bread. The cycle, of which eating bread is part, may be said to begin – though in a sense a cycle has no beginning – when a grain of wheat is sown. Think of that seed – small and hard and to the eye lifeless. But let it touch a crumb of moist humus and it will germinate, come to life, put out roots, sucking and clutching at the soil, drawing up water and potash and nitrogen and phosphates, not to mention iron and magnesium and copper and how many other trace elements, standing up, tall and slender, green and beautiful, to wave in the sunshine and at last to bring forth a hundred-fold. Then, when the old seed's separate existence has come to an end, some of the new grain is ground and baked and eaten by a man who turns part of it into energy, which he may use in various ways – to write poetry or to pray or to build a bridge or to plant potatoes – or perhaps to blow up his neighbour or to peddle drugs. And the part he does not use for these noble or devilish purposes, he would, if he lived in India, return to the soil; in this country it is likely to be washed out to sea. In either case, some seed will go back to the soil and the cycle will go on.

Thus the grain's cycle of life and death leads by man's intervention to a transformation of lifeless mineral matter into vegetable life and thence into human energy, thought and will-power, which in their turn can be used for creation or destruction, to make beauty or to kill a fellow creature. This process is surely sacred, miraculous – something far more surprising than anything in science fiction. It repeats within a few months all the millions of years of creation during which mineral, plant and animal evolved-and at last human will with its freedom. We take it for granted, but bread represents life and death and birth, the exchange which continues today between the different stages in the cycle of creation; it speaks for man's co-operation in partnership with God; it illustrates the contribution made by every stage of creation to the choice of good and evil. But if you thought such thoughts with every mouthful you ate, you would be a terrible bore at table. We do indeed partake of the body of the Lord every time we break bread. But we do not say so; by a sacramental act we set aside a representative moment to commemorate this – and, let me emphasize, much else too – a meaning too deep and too full for ordinary mortals to carry in the forefront of consciousness every minute of the day.

This brings us nearer to a constructive way of dealing with the paradoxes with which we began. It is part of Christianity's joyous assertion that life has meaning and that the creation is good. It is in stark contradiction to the Manichaean and the Buddhist distaste for matter and it links up with the Affirmative Way and the conviction that every flower and stone as well as every man-made tool and instrument has a message of its own. It is no less sharply in contrast with dialectical materialism and with a recent empirical theory of morals which was summarized in this statement:[1]

> The sense of the world must lie outside the world. In the world, everything is as it is and happens as it does happen. In it there is no value – and if there were it would be of no value. If there is any value which is of value it must lie outside all happening and being so. For all happening and being so is accidental.

This is the dreary conclusion reached in his *Tractatus* by Wittgenstein and let me note in passing that it seems to me entirely subjective, evolved from the inner consciousness and just as incapable of *proof* – in a Euclidean police-court sense – as any of my conclusions. It denies all meaning or interest to history, to art, to music, to human existence. It was Wittgenstein also who wrote that:

> 'Philosophy is a battle against the bewitchment of our intelligences by means of language.'

– which seems to me an excellent way of making a start with

philosophy, provided you do not forget its eventual purpose. What kind of philosophy would it be that did not love wisdom? The linguistic philosophers – against whom I rejoice to hear that the tide is beginning to turn – seemed to me like a man who sets out one afternoon in spring to spread a net over the raspberries to keep out the birds, but who becomes so engrossed in picking out the twigs and fircones and fragments of bindweed left in his net from last year that, when darkness falls, the raspberries are still uncovered – and he is himself hopelessly entangled in the net.

It is refreshing, as against these lexicographers, to consider the existentialist philosophers, not because they are always right but because they are at least trying to answer questions worth asking. The centre of their position, as I understand it, is that man determines the nature of his own existence, though he likes to pretend that he is forced to do what in fact he chooses to do. Sartre, for example, argues that unless a man can persuade himself that he must, let us say, go to the office five days a week, he will be faced by an agony of indecision as to what he *shall* do and a neurotic anxiety that he is not realizing his full potential. Like all heresies, this contains a truth. Man *is* unhappy when he is not realizing what he might be. St Augustine made the point long ago: 'Thou hast made us for Thyself and our heart is restless until it finds rest in Thee.' And Sartre is right in recognizing this uneasiness, this *Angst*, this anguished anxiety, but mistaken in not perceiving its true nature; it is due to a lack of harmony between man's soul and the universe. Sartre is right in denying the extreme determinist position of those who believe that man has no power to decide what he is or what he shall do. He is right in thinking that man is responsible for what he becomes. Where he is wrong is in denying the point on which Duns Scotus and Hopkins laid much stress – that there is an inscape, an essence if you like, a proper function, a full potential, for each object and person. Give it the right conditions and the rose may do its own thing, fulfil the law of its own being, come as near as it can to being a perfect example of its own species or variety. But even a rose has choice and may go wrong. I have seen the main shoot of a climbing rose burrowing into a ventilator on the side of a house and trying to hide from the light. And for man too there is a potential, for man in general and for each individual man, something special to himself but capable of infinite growth.

Here Nokes may ask apprehensively whether this means he must be always living his life at full stretch. You will remember that Nokes, like most of us, is neither a saint nor a genius. And there the analogy of the body comes in and the sacramental principle. You do not train a race-horse by keeping him all day at full gallop. An athlete can be over-trained and may be so fine-drawn that he lacks physical staying-power and, perhaps more seriously, the mental reserves, the calm confidence, he is going to need at the time of supreme trial; he may become nervous and irritable. For most people, I suspect, it is the same with the spirit. You set aside moments when you are at full stretch. A man who is sure of his wife's love may kiss her goodbye and go about his business all day without anxiety, just remembering her from time to time. And it is so in traditional Christian-ity. It is called 'habitual recollection'.[2] You set aside certain times, both public and private, when you try as hard as you can, and then go about your business like Sir Jacob Astley with his famous prayer before the battle of Edgehill: 'O Lord! thou knowest how busy I must be this day: if I forget thee, do not thou forget me.' Both Sir Jacob and the suburban husband have expressed their faith and love at the proper moments and do not have to be incessantly chattering and worrying. But they will both remember now and then.

Stop to think of the present moment. It has gone already in one tick of the clock; already it has become the past; it has ceased to exist. Yet your moment of consciousness and mine extend some way backwards and to a lesser extent forwards. The needle on a record-player moves on and the sound it is making at this instant has gone as soon as the ear has picked up the waves, but there would be no tune if the human consciousness had no memory of the notes just played nor anticipation of those to come. The mind can be trained to a longer period of consciousness that will enable it to understand a piece of music more complicated than a simple repeating tune; it can be trained to remember the argument in a long discourse and follow the speaker or writer in a sequence of thought. But if you can extend the period of conscious attention by training and an act of will, you can also suspend your attention, from idleness or frivolity or deliberate choice or simply because an image occurs to the brain that is more attractive than what the speaker is saying. Or you can 'find a moment'[3] – as Sir Jacob feared he would not – for recollection. To find a moment – how engaging a phrase! What a delightful thing to find! It will not last long; it will be gone as soon as it has come. But, when you find it, you can, if you like, set it aside for as long as your consciousness will hold it, as a sacramental moment, a moment that represents the passing of time, the coming of death, the stillness of eternity, your deepest faith. It is the sacrament of the present moment, of this passing moment. Now it has gone. While you are in time, it will never come again.

Let us go back to Nokes. There is another point on which he may be comforted. To realize the full personality need not mean intellectual distinction. It does of course mean using such reason as one possesses without being idle about it, but most of us can remember people who were intellectually free from complication – even what is generally called 'not very bright' – and who yet seemed *holy*, perhaps because of a simple delight in flowers or birds and love for other people, always, I am sure, because of a fundamental forgetfulness of self. Forgetfulness of self is not denial of the self and for those to whom it is given may be the best way of realizing the self.

Nor does the concept of sacramentalism rule out joy in the bare fact of existence. I have long treasured an African's criticism of the hurry and scurry of Europeans: 'When', he asked, 'do you ever see one of them sit under a tree and breathe air?' To breathe air, when you come to think of it, is almost as astonishing an experience as to eat bread; nothing induces panic so quickly as being unable to breathe, yet we take for granted the steady rhythm of inhaling the gas in which our planet is enfolded, absorbing it into the blood and using it for our own varied purposes. But the African meant that simply to sit still and breathe – without pondering about it – was good in itself. And surely he was right; it is part of my general argument that nearly all of us do live on different levels at different times and that at certain levels it is good to take pleasure in the mere fact of breathing air. For man is amphibious in two worlds, the animal world and the visible world of mind, intuition and spirit. In the animal world, he can praise God simply by existing happily, like Christopher Smart's cat, Jeoffry,

... who is the servant of the Living God, duly and daily serving him.
For at the first glance of the glory of God in the East he worships in his way.
... This is done by wreathing his body seven times round with elegant quickness.
For he knows that God is his Saviour ...

And it is a step beyond that to rejoice without second thoughts in a simple thing well done, a row of strawberries well planted or a hedge well cut and laid. But of course these are not the peaks; in a loved person to whom a man is wholly committed, he will be aware also at certain moments of the full inscape of the person, not doing anything, just existing, burning like the flame of a candle.

You will remember that Nokes has what he calls 'his moments' – moments of illumination and revelation – and that he wanted a system of belief to link them together and perhaps increase their frequency. This is what sacramentalism will do. Not only that, it will keep him sane and human and protect him against over-exposure. It is one aspect of what I have called elsewhere Blougramism[4] – fitting oneself to live in *this* world, which:

> ... by your leave
> Is Rome or London – not Fool's-Paradise.

As Blougram said:

> Under a vertical sun, the exposed brain
> And lidless eye and disemprisoned heart
> Less certainly would wither up at once
> Than mind confronted with the truth of Him.

But a sacrament we can endure. Air makes life possible and so does the sacramental principle,[5]

> Whereas did air not make
> This bath of blue and slake
> His fire, the sun would shake,
> A blear and blinding ball
> With blackness bound, and all
> The thick stars round him roll
> Flashing like flecks of coal,
> Quartz-fret or sparks of salt,
> In grimy vasty vault.

Here, then, I suggest, is a Christian principle which is joyous and affirmative and which can generally be applied in dealings with people. A person, whoever he is, is the visible sign of an invisible truth; he is a sign of the Incarnation. You may not remember that all the time but in a moment of decision about how he is to be treated, it is a help to call it to mind. It must be wrong for me to treat a person in such a way as to hinder the realization of all he might become, to make use of him for the purposes of my own idolatry.

But there are some other principles to be linked with sacramentalism.

2   AN ODE TO THE HUMDRUM

One of these I mentioned in the first interlude. I said that for me any theology must account for the fact that a Cox's Orange Pippin is better—in any sense of that word that I can understand—than a crab-apple from the hedge. The point is put in a story, of which there are other variants, told me long ago by an Afrikaner, really as a joke, to illustrate the independent nature of his people. One of them had occupied an untamed area in the *veldt* and had there built a house, with stables and cowstalls and pigsties, orchards, pastures and fields of mealies. A new pastor of the Dutch Reformed Church came to visit him and the farmer proudly showed him all he had done. The pastor congratulated him and added: 'But I'm sure you know that in all this the Lord is your partner and of course you don't forget to thank him for his share in the work.' 'Of course,' said the farmer, and then after a moment's hesitation, he added: 'But, Dominie, you should have seen this place when the Lord was farming it by himself.'

It is a more profound story, I think, than my informant meant it to be, implying the essential Christian point that man was given free will and invited to share in the creative labour of the universe. And this leads to another principle that with increasing complexity—both in the world and in the individual life—there are constant opportunities for growth which always carry risks of degradation. The old question about whether you would prefer to be a contented pig or a discontented philosopher admits of only one answer. You must leave the sty for the study and take the risk not only of discontent, and even anguish of mind, but of complete failure as a person—failure in marriage, let us say, or habitual drunkenness – risks which the pig did not have to face.

When a stone age people come into contact with a complex modern society, some of them may eventually achieve a richer and fuller life, but they always lose something and often some of them are plunged into shocking degradation. Indeed, our great-grandfathers used to comfort themselves with the belief that it was a law of nature that such people should perish in the face of what they called 'the higher races'; they would die, they thought, of a kind of cultural despair, a loss of the will to live, leading to group suicide. The Maoris seemed to them a perfect example of this theory but by the beginning of this century the Maoris had reversed the trend to group suicide and are now more numerous than before the coming of Europeans. But they do, I think, still illustrate my principle that while a greater complexity of culture may lead for some to real gains – not merely material gains but a richer human life – it will also almost certainly involve loss and misery.

There can, as I say, be only one answer; we must as a general rule be ready to come out of the Garden of Eden and accept the knowledge of good and evil, the risks and hopes of the more complex and dangerous position. Take a plunge, start a new career, take up a new subject, widen the possibilities. But with that adventurous advice I must associate a divergent principle, very unfashionable today. In an earlier chapter I included a brief hymn to hypocrisy. Let me now add an ode in praise of the institution, of habit, of routine, of the humdrum organization which keeps things moving. It will often seem to the young repellent. They feel it is constricting; how much better, they say, if you could be free from marriage, the Church, the state – with all their rules and pretences. If you channel your personal effort into an institution, they will say, you are narrowing the boundless scope of your energies, hampering yourself with all kinds of tiresome formalities, clogging the impetus of your imagination by the slow patient business of persuading other people. But in fact – I would argue – not only is the institution usually a convenient – and sometimes the only – way of getting what you are aiming at but you may find that it does also provide enriching experiences at which you had not even guessed. You cannot play a Beethoven symphony by yourself and you cannot hear it unless someone has got an orchestra together and raised the money to appoint a musical director and engaged a concert hall. If you take part in a local orchestra or even an enterprise to start one, there may be boring work on committees but there may be friendship too and you will become aware of new interpretations of familiar beauties.

You may wish to make sure your daughter's education includes nothing you disapprove of and you may think it would be nice to educate her yourself – but for that you really need an enchanted island, a Caliban to split the logs and an Ariel for more delicate work, quite apart from the psychological problems your Miranda is likely to face when she meets her Ferdinand and has to disengage from her Prospero. It is likely to be not only more convenient but actually better to send her to school and you may find, not only for her but for yourself, new vistas opening through a parents' association or something of the kind and also in what your daughter brings back with her to you. You have to circumscribe and define your glorious but not very precise desire for education; you have to reject some possibilities and prefer others and make your plan fit into a society.

You may 'want to write', but – unless you are an unusual genius – you won't get very far until you have established some means of keeping body and soul together, determined to set aside regular times for work and given some thought to the public you are writing for. You will need an agent and a publisher and may even find it useful to listen to their advice. Once again, you have to reduce the infinite number of choices open to you and concentrate on a narrower front. And, in one respect, what is usually called prayer, thought about God, is very like writing. Unless he makes rules about it and sets aside special times, the ordinary man will find there is always something else to do and will not get very far.

Marriage is another example. You may think that too will limit and confine you. Many have thought so — and it is true that Christian marriage limits the possibilities open to you; it will not let you take another wife or desert your first. You cannot just walk out after a quarrel and abandon all responsibility. For most people it means you cannot afford luxuries you could when you were single. You take a package deal for life — for better for worse, for richer for poorer, in sickness and in health. You take a risk when you give each other enforceable rights; you undertake the joint care of children. If you approach marriage with an eye to what you can get out of it, your marriage lines will be just a piece of paper. But if you really commit yourself to marriage and want to give, then the relationship may grow into new dimensions that would only rarely be possible in a liaison that was not consciously vowed to permanence. You lose your single life; you may find a better one.

Those who made early experiments with the power of steam faced the problem of turning into continuous motion the first forward kick of the piston when steam filled the cylinder. How were they to get the piston back? Their answer was the fly-wheel, a wheel with a heavy rim which, once it was moving, would carry the piston back to its first position ready for the next impulse.[6] It takes a little extra energy to get it moving but it stores energy and makes movement continuous. The wills and affections of sinful men, undirected, are as powerless as steam escaping into the atmosphere; directed into a narrow channel like a cylinder, they need the regulating weight of rules and institutions to carry on the effect of one impulse to the next.

10

Fourth Interlude: Interlocking Opposites

1 THE SECOND LOOK

We have been talking in terms of metaphor; there is no other way with such a subject. We spoke of sacramentalism, of a scale between sacramentalism and a Manichaean rejection of matter, of another scale between sacramentalism and idolatry, and of sacramentalism, as a principle good in itself and affording a healthy release from tension. We spoke of the divergent possibilities that come with increased complexity and then of the necessity to channel energy into an institution that will store energy from one impulse to the next like a fly-wheel. Let me add another metaphor to the armoury we are accumulating. Let us call it, since it has to be called something, The Second Look, but the name is not altogether satisfactory. It has to do with the kind of situation that most people have sometimes faced, when two lines of conduct present themselves, so closely linked that sometimes both seem wrong and sometimes both seem right. Yet on the face of it they are opposed; they are mutually contradictory. But they are interlocking opposites.

Sometimes the difficulty arises directly out of the nature of human institutions. There is always a three-fold aspect. Mediaeval writers on spiritual matters sometimes overdid their desire to find a trinity-in-unity in every aspect of man's behaviour. They symbolized the principle in daily actions:[1]

> I the Trinity illustrate,
> > Drinking watered orange pulp–
> In three sips the Arian frustrate;
> > While he drains his in one gulp!

But it is not merely a rhetorical device to see in a human institution such as marriage or the church three essential parts—creation, embodiment, an ongoing spirit. There is the first creative thought; there is the embodiment of that thought in action, in rules, customs or laws; finally there is the continuing spirit in which the institution operates. However admirable the creative thought, its embodiment is subject to human limitations; the spirit guides but men may misinterpret. There is always a narrow path to walk and sometimes a stark choice between adherence to the original concept and a radical re-thinking.

When Jesus was walking in Galilee, the Jewish establishment—the high priest and his family and adherents, the whole ruling priestly caste—were faced with an insoluble political dilemma. They could neither rid themselves of Roman rule nor acquiesce in Rome's tolerant, worldly and mildly superstitious pagan spirit. They took refuge in the strict letter of a minutely punctilious code of conduct and ceremony. Against this, Jesus directed much of his teaching. He was insistent that rigid legalism was not enough. But not a letter of the law was to pass away. There we face the interlocking opposites. His disciples are to keep the law. But they are to keep it in spirit and, if this often means that they must go much further than the law demands, it also means that when human need demands they may break its letter. They must, in short, treat it sacramentally, respecting what it stands for but not idolatrously bowing down before outward observance.

Today the danger is reversed; the prevailing mood is certainly not one of strict observance to the letter of the law. It is rather anarchic. But anarchy—insistence that the convenience of the moment should be considered rather than any general rule—does often lead to an unhappiness and perhaps to a degradation, not less than anything likely to arise from keeping the law too strictly.

Not long ago I heard on the radio the case of a young woman who had two step-children and two children of her own. After her second child was born, she went through a period of deep depression, due, no doubt, in part to physical exhaustion, and partly to having too much to cope with and probably to not enough support from her husband, though she did not say that. When she became pregnant again, all her friends urged her to have the pregnancy terminated – the polite way of telling her that she should kill her unborn child. She understood their arguments; she agreed that it would have been better if the child had not been conceived. But it was *her* child; it was part of herself. She resented their advice; still more she resented the burden of choice which a recent change in the law placed on her shoulders. She was so young and inexperienced. She felt that she ought not to have to decide; someone wiser than herself ought to *know* what was right and what was wrong; the law should tell her what to do.

It was too much for her – the terrible burden of freedom – and we are back with Ivan's parable about the Grand Inquisitor. The Inquisitor, you will remember, thought that Jesus had given the wrong answers to that wise and dread spirit who had tempted him in the desert. He ought not – said the Inquisitor – to have given us freedom. The girl on the radio would have agreed with him and she *seemed* to imply – though perhaps I read this into what she said – a deeper criticism than she actually expressed of the society in which she found herself. She clearly wanted to be told that it would be wrong to have the abortion that her friends advised, but she also implied that she had been left without rules or guidance or standards at an earlier stage in her story. She had had too much freedom all the way.

Today we are all in favour of freedom and so of course we think the Grand Inquisitor a heretic. But, like all heretics, he had seen a truth. If freedom means no rules at all, it does lead to misery; it makes men slaves to indecision and anxiety – the *Angst* on which the existentialists lay such stress – just as legalism makes them slaves to rules they feel

foreign to themselves. There is always a knife-edge between legalism and anarchy. Consider how complex are
the issues raised by the girl on the radio about abortion.
To kill an unborn child is murder; it is destroying potential
life. That child might be Beethoven or Shakespeare. That
was something that she herself obscurely felt. And then to
make abortion easy contributes to a general feeling that
man is not responsible for his actions, that difficulties can
always be got over, that everything will come right in the
end, that nothing matters but what you can get away with.

But if the law permits abortion only when it is necessary
to save the life of the mother, the law will drive it under-
ground, into sleazy little back rooms, to be performed by
greasy old men, unclean and unskilful. And if that way is not
taken, it will seem to many cruel to enforce the unhappiness
that will result if the child is born and continues to be unwanted. The girl on the radio said very little about her
husband but it seemed that he was among those who wanted
her to kill the child. Should she part with him on that issue?
Perhaps he would come to love the child when it was born,
but perhaps he would make it feel unwanted. Ought she to
give up the chance of making her husband more deeply
and truly human – of 'sanctifying' him, as Paul said of the
woman married to an unbeliever?

For the legislator today the dilemma is a hard one – but
for the would-be Christian, if it is his own personal life that
is involved, the answer may be much more clear. He or she
must step back from the dilemma into which the unhappy
girl and the legislator have got themselves and think out
the situation from the beginning in terms of principle
balanced against human need. If man and woman always
came together in a spirit that I would call sacramental, they
would not want to kill the unborn child. But we are self-
willed and imperfect and of course we know that preg-
nancies will often occur which on all human assumptions
seem likely to cause unhappiness. When that does happen,
there can be no question of the general principle that the

child should be welcomed and given all the love and care that can be mustered. That principle may lead to a very hard decision. It may be that one of the partners cannot see the situation in such terms and this may reveal so different a view of their whole relationship, so different a view of life and its meaning, that the other may come to see that it is the relationship, not the child, which ought to be killed. Yet until this question arose, it may be that each of the two would have described the marriage they hoped for in much the same terms. But one was thinking of comfort, happiness, prosperity, the other of the kind of love which is ready to give something up.

The teaching of the gospels becomes easier to understand if one thinks of a knife-edge between lines of conduct which may appear similar but turn out to be divergent or which may appear opposite but prove complementary. In either case, they demand a second look from a new standpoint. This is not the middle way between two extremes which was the Greek ideal of conduct; the two courses are not extremes and may even appear very similar.

Consider the second temptation in the desert. It would be wrong to float down from the Temple supported by angels because it would be tempting God, taking Him for granted, making use of Him. But if you have faith, you can throw mountains into the sea. It sounds contradictory. Throwing mountains into the sea is not a very sensible occupation unless you have some special purpose in mind. It is not very different from floating down from the Temple. Where does tempting God end and trusting God begin? We can all think of people who by sheer faith have, as we say, achieved miracles, moved mountains. That vigorous picturesque expression has no doubt usually been taken metaphorically. It implies, though characteristically the implication is not stated, that faith should be used for proper ends and with full consideration. Today man—working like the Afrikaner farmer in partnership with the Lord and on the basis of faith, though often a faith held by his fathers and grandfathers rather than directly by himself—*can* throw mountains into the sea. But he should not undertake it lightly. His earth-moving machinery may involve all kinds of changes in the balance of nature, and these must be thought out as well as the finance and the logistics of feeding the workers.

It is a commonplace that Jesus answered awkward questions by shifting the ground of the argument and saying: You are looking at the whole question in the wrong light. But even when he was not answering questions, his teaching seems again and again to demand interpretation in the light of that pattern. The rich fool is reproved for building new barns for his crops, but it is wrong to start building a tower unless you have counted the cost; the contradiction is not resolved but avoided if one steps back, takes a second look and considers the context of each of these sayings. The rich fool's mistake was not in counting the cost and looking ahead but in the colloquy with his soul. He said to his soul that he would spend the rest of his life feasting and enjoying good things—which is not only idolatry but taking mercy for granted. The metaphor of the tower is invoked in what appears to be just the opposite sense but it is really consistent. You would be a fool to build a tower without counting the cost; you know that and it is the same in spiritual matters. It is no use thinking you can follow me without counting the cost. And this is really what St Augustine meant with his 'Dilige et quod vis fac'—'Make your choice lovingly and with care and make sure that what you have chosen is what you really love—what you will make a sacrifice for—and then you need not bother too much about rules; act with that choice in mind and you will not go wrong.'

There is an apocryphal story of a saying of Jesus, not included in the gospels, no doubt because the evidence that he actually said it was not good enough. But it is in keeping with the tradition of the developing church. He saw a man working in the fields on the Sabbath and said that, if the man knew he was breaking the Sabbath, there was hope for him but if he did not know he was beyond the pale. Not to know – in that age, in Palestine – meant he was cut off from human kind, an anti-social heretic and idolater. But if he knew what he was doing, he had made up his mind, no doubt for sufficient reason, and because he looked on rules in their proper light. Choose what you really love and then do as your heart tells you – exactly.

2 THE AMPHIBIANS

I have several times used the word amphibious or amphibian.[2] Neither the word nor the idea is original. But the idea is much older than the word. Man is an exile on a pilgrimage to God but also he is a citizen in his father's house, who rejoices in his citizenship. He is an animal but also a spirit. For some people, a sense of this dual citizenship increases as they grow older. It was expressed at a recent memorial service:[3]

> One of the many pleasures of being old and nearing one's end is to wake up in the night round about 3 a.m. – the favourite dying time, as I understand – feeling half in and half out of one's body, so that it seems quite a toss-up whether you make off or return for another day. In that situation one is aware, in an almost tangible way, of being between Time and Eternity with an extraordinary vivid sense of the beauty of the earth – its shapes and colours and smells – and of earthly life, our human loves and work and procreation, all the golden hours of mortality.
>
> At the same time, an equally vivid certainty of being, as an infinitesimal particle of God's creation, a participant in His purposes for it, which are loving and not destructive, universal and not particular.

That sense of being amphibious between time and

eternity has occurred to many people throughout their lives. To call it 'amphibious' is of course only a metaphor though a useful one; I want now to explore it further.

There was once talk of the Great Chain of Being and the Principle of Plenitude. The ideas were used to justify the existence of evil. A perfect world must be full and must include everything that possibly could exist. Scorpions exist – so they are possible. If they did not exist, something possible would be left out and the world would be imperfect. This accounts for the existence of things most men do not like, scorpions and mosquitoes, earthquakes and cancer. The idea is formal, mathematical, unreal. It is not a way of thinking that appeals to us much today. But from the general idea of a world that must be *full* in order to be perfect, it followed that there must be a *continuous* Chain of Being with the slug and the earwig fairly low in the biological scale and man at the top. This was pre-Darwinian and pre-Mendelian thought and I mention it partly as a curiosity but mainly because it contributed to the Victorian idea of Progress. That too is discredited. We have seen in this century not only unequalled horrors of cold-blooded cruelty but the squandering of forests, of the earth's surface, of our stored mineral energy. We have seen emptiness of heart, the greed of affluence, the hollowness of materialism. We can hardly think we have made much direct progress lately. But looked at in terms of biological time, still more of geological time, there can be no serious doubt that progress has taken place. From protozoa to fish, from fish to mammals, there has been continual movement towards something more complex – and this process somehow produced Mind – intellect, will, self-consciousness, the appreciation of beauty; self-sacrifice for a cause or a person; the dedication of the self to knowledge or healing; laughter; reverence and awe; all the divine best in man. These qualities were not born in a flash, overnight; they emerged from the evolutionary process, which took millions and millions of years, yet they run clean counter to what we think of as its methods; the mystic, the mathematician and the poet are less likely to escape the sabre-toothed tiger than the sharp aggressive fellow with all his wits about him. The best qualities in man are much *more* than are needed for survival.

Thus, at the stage in the cosmic process that most concerns us, the emergence of mind, there seems to be a discontinuity in the methods of nature. Once we needed ruthless aggression to survive; now we need wise co-operation. Indeed, there was discontinuity before the emergence of mind. The Great Chain of Being is fiction. There is a discontinuity between gas, mud, rock and crystal on the one hand and life on the other; in spite of intermediate forms, there is a discontinuity between vegetable life and animal life.

Our grandfathers were impressed with the ruthlessness of nature, the ferocity with which the fittest survived at the expense of the less fit. But even among the animals, before the appearance of man, there were clues as to the direction of the next step. It was only rarely among reptiles, insects and fish that much concern was shown for the safety of their young. But among birds and mammals it was the general rule to feed and care for the young and in many species the female was often prepared to risk, or even give up, her life for them. This selflessness emerged from the evolutionary process by 'natural' means but was quite contrary to the ruthless individualism that seemed to characterize the process in its earlier aspects. And a second clue emerged among the more intelligent species, a readiness to co-operate for a common purpose, strong in the hunting species but also among some of the eaters of grass. Self-sacrifice and co-operation — these are instinctively human characteristics, or so we think. But they appear as clues before the appearance of humans. Let us however go back to the amphibians.

The amphibians in the literal biological sense were a step forward from the fish; in human, metaphorical terms, they were an experiment. By coming out of the water—more than two hundred million years ago—they increased the possibilities of life. What an adventure! *They* did not know, of course, that it was an adventure; they could not foresee all that would come, all to which their first squirming steps would contribute. But they, inhabitants of two fluids, were a stage in the process which led to mind, something quite beyond their range. And why should we suppose that we can foretell the further developments of conscious mind any more than they could then? We are faintly and intermittently aware of an amphibious element in our lives; a few mystics have had experiences of a state of being which to them was utterly real but of which they can convey very little to us. There is for example that moment when St Augustine was talking to his mother, shortly before her death :[4]

> ' ... our thoughts ranged over the whole compass of material things in their various degrees, up to the heavens themselves, from which the sun and the moon and the stars shine down upon the earth. Higher still we climbed, thinking and speaking all the while in wonder at all that you have made. At length we came to our own souls and passed beyond them to that place of everlasting plenty where you feed your people for ever with the food of truth. There life is that Wisdom by which all these things that we know are made ... And while we spoke of the eternal Wisdom, longing for it and straining for it with all the strength of our hearts, for one fleeting instant we reached out and touched it. And we sighed, and abandoning on that far shore those first fruits of the spirit, we fell back to the sound of our own voices, and the determinate words of human discourse ... '

We—most of us—can know very little of that far shore. Should we not therefore be content to be agnostic? Well, we are better equipped than the frogs or the lung-fishes; we can make a guess at the *direction* of development. We have clues. There were clues, as the mammals developed, to the development of man, the beginnings of self-sacrifice and co-operation; here, in the vision of St Augustine and St Monica, there is perhaps a clue to the next stage. If you can believe that a spinning ball of gas and fire could in the course of millions and millions of years produce 'by pure chance' Shakespeare and a peacock and all the pulsating marvels of man's body and the heavens, you can believe anything. Personally I find it much easier to believe in a purpose and a direction, though far beyond my comprehension. So far, there have been aeons of hardly perceptible change followed by periods of far more rapid development, each taking place in a new stage as though the creation had so to speak changed gear. One such new stage of development came with mind. The arrival of mind has produced a demand for new qualities if we are to survive. It also suggests that mere survival is not enough. All this indicates the probability of another stage. Surely it is sensible to suppose that it will be a move in the direction in which we are most different from the animals, just as they are different from mud and rock. The cosmic process that discarded the dinosaur has now produced Leonardo da Vinci and Michelangelo. We should be desperate indeed to suppose it would go back to the dinosaur. We may destroy ourselves in our own greed and folly but if there is to be another stage it will surely be a move towards a greater capacity for the love of beauty and wisdom, for the joy and pain of making something, for the kind of love for someone else which overcomes evolutionary self-love.

Now I suppose that an exceptionally gifted dog might have a momentary glimpse of human methods of apprehension as far beyond his normal range as St Augustine's moment of divine apprehension was beyond *his*.[5] But I am not suggesting the possibility of another species as different from me as I am from the dog, though biology unaided might lead one to some such surmise. By an act of choice, I believe that:[6]

> ... at a predetermined moment, a moment in time
> and of time,
> A moment not out of time, but in time, in what we call
> history: transecting, bisecting the world of time, a
> moment in time but not like a moment of time ...

there was a revelation of eternal Light. If Christians are right in that belief, it is not by further biological change that we must expect clearer understanding of that Light but by entering a new timeless dimension. What that will be like we can understand no more than those first amphibians understood the world they entered, when they emerged, blinking and shaking their heads, from the primeval ocean.

3　IRONY

In this chapter we have been concerned with linked opposites, with the need for a second look at them, with living simultaneously in air and water, time and eternity. To complete the series, let us think of the need for irony. It is part of the multiple nature of truth and takes us back to a point I made at the beginning, that a lark may be proclaiming its right to its territory and *also* the glory of God. Neither proclamation excludes the other; it depends on the audience. Both the ornithologist and the poet are right. So we can look on the story of the Garden of Eden as a myth and at the same time as a psychological truth.

When I speak of irony, I am not thinking of humour, laughter and play, which are all part of the Christian tradition.[7] They are to be found in both Judaism and Hellenism, the parents of Christianity. 'As a signet of an emerald set in a work of gold, so is the melody of music with pleasant wine', wrote the author of Ecclesiasticus and a little later enjoins his hearer to get up early and go to work 'but get

thee home without delay. There take thy pastime and do
what thou wilt ... ' Aristotle thought that 'Recuperative
rest and cheerful play seem to be necessary for life', and
St Thomas Aquinas that Christianity combined the two
traditions. He wrote that: 'unmitigated seriousness betokens
a lack of virtue because it wholly despises play, which is as
necessary for a good human life as rest is.' And he recounts
an ancient story of someone who had seen St John the
Apostle as an old man playing 'like a boy' with a tame
partridge. It may seen solemn, pompous, lacking in humour
even to mention this – and so it would be if it had not at
various periods of history been thought proper to pull a long
face at the mention of religion and indeed to wear a long
face all day – an attitude that seems to me Manichaean and
blasphemous because it denies the goodness of the creation.

But irony is quite different from play, from relaxation
and enjoyment.[8] It lies somewhere in a border country
between contradictions and thus it is essential to Christian
life, which is both joyful and serious, joyful because of the
Incarnation and serious because of suffering and because
we are responsible for our actions. In that border country,
laughter is never far from a feeling that there is something
a little frightening about what is not fully understood.
Primitive people ritualize aspects of life that they feel are at
the same time important and mysterious, such as birth,
adolescence, marriage and death. We tend to hide them in
embarrassed laughter. The ritual illness of the father when
the wife is in labour – the couvade – surely expresses the
same feeling as the *Punch* joke about the doctor who had
never lost a father yet. It is obviously a difficult stage in a
woman's life when she transfers her main loyalty from her
parents to a husband and for him too there is a delicate path
to be trodden. Some primitive peoples escape the situation
by a ritual prohibition of meeting between husband and
mother-in-law; we make it a music-hall joke. 'Hortense,
Hortense, how can you giggle at a moment like this?' says
an enthusiastic amorist in the *New Yorker*, and thousands

of jokes about sex turn on nothing more than the contrast between the solemn and the flippant. There would be nothing to laugh at if there was not a feeling that sexual relations really are among the most serious things in life. But poor Hortense had to giggle because of the portentous solemnity of her admirer and because she knew that she ought to be feeling something she was not. She felt like the schoolgirl who giggles in church.

That kind of laughter is still not irony. It is an escape from inadequacy. The person who laughs feels inadequate to the situation confronting him, and may also feel that the situation itself is inadequate to what it demands. He is uneasy because he does not understand something immensely serious. The primitive tries to make it impersonal by ritual. Growing up is not just something that happens to me and only to me, he says; it is universal. Let us play it out before a new audience, before the gods, before the ancestors and the unborn. The modern giggler is also picturing, perhaps unconsciously, a new but more intimate audience, to whom what is happening will seem absurd. And with this idea of a second audience we begin to draw closer to true irony, in which there is always a consciousness of a second audience.

The essence of true irony is an appeal from one audience to another, to an inner audience as well as an outer, as in the Greek play, where the spectators knew the myth on which the play was based. They would draw a sharp breath of horror at words with which the hero unconsciously foretold his own dreadful fate, while to the characters on the stage, who were not supposed to know what was going to happen, the same words would carry only their superficial meaning. Words uttered in irony may pass as trivial to one hearer, but to another, more sensitive or better informed, they will carry a deeper significance and set up a bond of intimacy between the speaker and the one who understands. H. J. Fowler, trying to define irony, pointed out that sometimes the dealer in irony is saying one thing outwardly but something else to another self in his own breast. It is of this last kind of irony that I am specially thinking. It may indicate arrogance – 'No one else is clever enough to know what I really mean' – or humility – 'I am not quite sure that in the last analysis what I am saying is not ridiculous'.

Why should we not recognize both these two human reactions to the mysterious and frightening nature of the most important experiences of life? Why should we not both ritualize like the primitive and laugh like the modern? Martin Thornton has written of the need for irony in connection with worship. Everything possible, he suggests, should be done with music, vestments, flowers and incense to make worship a perfect ritual but the worshipper should then recognize with a smile that to God the whole affair must seem childish and absurd.

But because the human condition is inextricably entangled in interlocking opposites, the need for irony is wider than this. The teaching of Jesus in parables was almost always ironic, in the sense of speaking to at least two audiences. One must suppose that, in the actual form in which they were uttered, the parables were often told as straightforward anecdotes of something that had happened in the neighbourhood. 'There was a man not far from here who scattered his seed all over the place, on the path, in the bushes and among the stones. And what happened to that good seed? ... ' As the tale of the sower is told in the gospels, the inner circle of disciples who need to have it explained seems to us rather obtuse. But, if told in the tone of voice I have suggested, a peasant audience would laugh at a man who wasted his seed so carelessly; there would be an outer audience who listened for entertainment only, who did not pay much attention to the inner meaning. That the intention was ironic is clear from the references which immediately follow to those who have ears to hear and to those who hear but do not understand. I think again of my own experience of Indian peasants. They were uneasy with abstract ideas and unfamiliar words but very quick indeed to understand the analogy between some tale or joke and a given situation. If anyone heard the story of the Good Samaritan and did not know what it was about, I have a feeling that he must have been wilful rather than obtuse.

Let me add a suggestion that there was often a double irony in the parables; peel away the literal meaning and there is an inner; peel away that and there is a third. The tale about the unjust steward is a good example. Again I interpret it in terms of a society I once knew well, where there were rich landowners with agents who were some-time dishonest and middle-class tenants who were always in arrears. Perhaps it began something like this: 'Have you heard about that rich man over at such-and-such a village and what happened when he found out that his agent was cheating him?' They had all heard something about it—but rumours only—and they crowded round to hear more. 'The agent knew he'd been found out and couldn't escape the sack. He had to show his accounts and get them audited. What was he to do? He wasn't prepared to give up being one of the middle class. He wasn't going to dig for a living or go round with a begging bowl. Of course he knew that most of the rich man's tenants owed him arrears of rent; perhaps there was a loan for a daughter's wedding or a postponement of rent because of bad luck when that sudden hailstorm slashed the crops. People always want time to pay up. He sent for them one by one and did a deal with each of them in turn, reducing the debt and giving them forged receipts to prove their case. And of course they were delighted and promised to give him a bed whenever he wanted for as long as he liked.' Here the Lord paused, and, looking at his hearers, went on: 'What a gang of crooks! And yet you've got to hand it to that agent. Think of the trouble he took and the risks he ran. Every false receipt he gave the tenants made his own account worse with his master. That's the kind of trouble people take and the lengths to which they'll go in *their* world—the world of rich men and their accounts and their fraudulent agents. What about us? We, who call ourselves decent folk, do we take as much trouble as that about the things we regard as important? Won't God ask to see our accounts?' And he went on to draw several distinct morals. Anyone who is concerned about 'the true riches', should take at least as much trouble about his spiritual progress as those who are concerned about money do about their affairs. 'And, since you have to handle money, you might as well learn something from this rascal of an agent and use it to make friends—because the goodwill of anyone, even a tenant prepared to cheat his landlord, is worth having and will be credited to your heavenly account. But don't think that *you* can behave as they do. If you are not scrupulously faithful with this earthly money, you will never be trusted with the true riches. You have to be quite clear which it is you really want; you have one allegiance. Your dealings with Mammon and the world of money must always come second and be used for a purpose of the other City of which you are a member, the Heavenly City.'

Was there another meaning behind that? In several of the parables, the owner of an estate or a vineyard clearly represents the Almighty, the vineyard is Israel and the currency in which men trade is the currency of Heaven, the true riches of this parable. If that kind of scheme were applied here too, the fraudulent agent would stand for the rulers of Israel—who are mentioned soon afterwards as taking the parable amiss—and the implication would be that they are to be admired for the diligence with which they go about their task, even though they are dealing in the wrong currency and cheating God by asking the people for payment in lip-service and formality instead of wholehearted obedience. Or again, look at the story in the light of the preaching of John the Baptist, that God would shortly demand his accounts from everyone, and link it with the facts—known to everyone—of the wealth of the Temple and the corruption that went on there. We know how this angered Jesus. 'You have made it a den of thieves!' he said. What did the rulers of Israel do about this? Did they

sit down, like the crooked agent, and wonder what to do?
Did they resolve, as he did, to redistribute more justly
their Master's wealth while there was still time? They
might have learnt that, even from him! I have a feeling that
that interpretation might have sprung to mind quite readily
in Palestine in A.D.30. But one interpretation need not rule
out another, any more than one interpretation of the lark's
song.

I quoted Martin Thornton on the need for irony in con-
nexion with worship. He has also suggested that all the
paradoxical sayings are to be interpreted with an inner
meaning and an outer, and always with consciousness of
man's absurdity—that is to say as irony. Let me quote:

> To find life we are to lose it; to love God we must
> hate parents and friends; to be rich we need to become
> poor; to reach maturity means to become as little
> children. Such an approach implies ... that a sense of
> humour is not barely permissible to religion but a
> profound religious quality: pride is the worst of the
> sins and the worst form of pride is to take oneself too
> seriously.

And in another passage he suggests that isolated sayings
of Jesus can always 'safely be regarded as irony' and what
we should do is to go behind them and seek a deeper
understanding of the divine personality—bearing in mind
always our own 'glorious absurdity'.

To summarize, the sayings of Jesus are usually the outer
sign of an inner truth and rooted in linked opposites. There
are several possible audiences, the wholly thoughtless and
superficial and those who see different layers of inner
meaning. There is always an inner audience in one's own
breast and—once you have lovingly made your choice of
Christianity—you may ask that inner audience how your
interpretation of this saying would appear to the Incarnate
Word. But you should also remember another audience of

those who for the last two thousand years have considered these sayings and how they should be interpreted. A sense of proportion, a sense of one's own smallness, an ability to perceive one's own absurdity, an awareness of the paradoxical contraries of life—these are among the implications of irony.

There is a prayer that expresses an attitude to the sorrows of the world as well as to intellectual questionings: 'Teach me to care and not to care'. There is also a simplicity beyond all irony. Singleness of heart is a virtue; so is simplicity of mind. Think as deeply as you can and then laugh at the absurdity of your thoughts in the face of eternity— and then is the time to take the head down into the heart, as the Russian Orthodox monks taught, to believe quite simply without question, to lose your doubts in the one certainty of a loving purpose.

The Heart of the Message

I NOBODADDY

We have been talking about how a Christian should behave, not about what he should believe. But I cannot altogether separate behaviour from belief; the one depends on the other.

So we must say something about belief and I propose to begin, for a change, by asking Nokes a question. 'What kind of God is it that you don't believe in?' If we press him, I think it will become clear that the God he does not believe in – the God he thinks I do believe in – is like Blake's 'old Nobodaddy up aloft', a negative being in every way, living in a temple with 'Thou Shalt Not' writ over the door, a jealous God angry with people who *sin* – a word Nokes does not much like – a God who is offended if human beings do not spend all their time standing in rows praising him. Well, I concede at once that I cannot believe in that kind of God either. The old jibe is half true and man did create God in his own image. He clothes with his own ideas his apprehension of an ultimate reality. But he does this afresh with each revolution of the human spirit. I do not think of God as the seventeenth century did nor the eighteenth nor the nineteenth. Blake's Nobodaddy starts from a very primitive Jewish concept of God, already out of date by the sixth century B.C. and the Babylonian captivity. Even that primitive concept has been coarsened in the form in which it soaked through to the popular mind in Northern Europe after the Reformation, when so often corrupt practices were cured only at the expense of losing

contact with the traditional wisdom and intellectual achieve-
ment of Christendom. The God Nokes does not believe in
is not really Christian at all, but the Gothic peasant's view
of a Semitic tribal deity.

What *do* I believe then? In the first place in a purpose. I
find it impossible to believe that it was 'by pure chance' that
a spinning ball of gas and fire should have produced *life*
and that life should have developed 'by pure chance' in
such a way as to produce *mind*. Julian Huxley–who did
believe it was all 'pure chance'–once calculated the odds
against the horse developing in just the shape we know
today. He found that the odds were so enormous that it
would take a book of five hundred pages to print the
noughts. And I suppose the odds would be of the same order
for every other creature–spider, toadstool, pheasant, fox;
primrose, cowslip, bluebell, foxglove; pike and stickleback
and the teeming millions of the voracious sea–and the
odds against the world evolving as it has done become far
beyond the possibility of any imagination. I think that 'pure
chance' is only a bad way of saying 'a purpose not yet understood'.

But, Nokes will ask, why do you suppose that the purpose
behind evolution is *loving*? The methods of evolution are
harsh and sometimes to us seem cruel. Sometimes the most
beautiful is the most destructive; think of the tiger, the
leopard, the peregrine falcon. Sometimes destruction is
utterly repulsive. Think of cancer, cholera, plague, the
long drawn out wasting diseases of the nervous system.
And of course I must answer in the sense of the last part of
the Book of Job; I was not there when the morning stars
sang together and all the sons of God shouted for joy. I
cannot deck myself with majesty and excellency nor array
myself with glory and beauty. There is a great deal I cannot
understand but, such as it is, I must use my understanding
so far as I can. I cannot resist adding that the God of fire
and tempest and creative energy who spoke to Job from the
whirlwind in such superb and tumultuous language approved

of the bitter things Job had said to him, of his questioning of Almighty purpose. Job could not understand but he had been right to ask his terrible questions and the three friends who had talked platitudes were reproved.[1] I cannot understand a great deal but I can form some opinion of the *direction* of the Purpose. I judge by what seems to me the best of what emerges at the stage of Mind. I judge by the nobility, the courage, the understanding of pain in Aeschylus and Sophocles and Plato; by Jewish awe at the splendour of the creation, by the Jewish conviction of the holiness of the purpose behind history; by the combination of these two traditions in the Christian tradition. In that I include Christian culture – all that Lord Clark calls Civilization – but I would add the best of the Hindu and Chinese and Muslim civilizations. When I look at all this I have a feeling of experiment, of probing. In the new dimension of Mind – of which after only five thousand years we are only just at the beginning – I see something like the experiments which produced dinosaurs and pterodactyls and then discarded these creatures in favour of blackbirds and lapwings and at last of tool-making mammals, who could draw pictures and laugh and love their children – and kill each other – who could make instruments for music – or for torture. In this new dimension, in a hundred different ways, man is allowed glimpses, here and there, of an Eternal Wisdom, some bright, some dim. These glimpses are allowed not only in the form of what is generally called religion but also in music or painting, in plays or novels. In this whole range of activities, there is experiment and perhaps our culture too is about to be discarded like the dinosaurs.

Here I must make a logical break. There is another line of thought which leads to the same conclusion. I also believe that there was one clear moment of revelation when the Light, the Purpose, broke through with a clarity so much more complete than anywhere else that it was of a different kind. This was when the Word became Flesh. A word is the outgoing of a thought; The Word is the outgoing of the Creative Thought or Purpose behind the universe. And since the Word was in the beginning with God, there must surely have been from the beginning a continual outgoing of the Word into the world. Socrates and the second Isaiah received inspiration from the same source as Augustine and Aquinas. This indeed Aquinas taught, but I would go further and argue that it was the same light that reached Buddha Gautama and the author of the *Bhagavad Gita*. Indeed, the spark that fired Voltaire to mock at what he thought infamous was divine, and Bertrand Russell must by now have been surprised to find himself at least for a moment on the threshold of Heaven. The scientist, whether he knows it or not, operates by the inspiration of the Word.

Thus two paths bring me to the same conclusion, that the purpose of life is creative spirit, expressed in man's freedom to make decisions, to feel compassion, to care for other people, to create beauty, in paint or sounds or words, by delight in the creation, by holiness of life. It does not matter that one of the two lines of thought arises from looking at what I know of the course of history while the other follows from the inspiration granted to the writer of St John's Gospel. Indeed I believe that the combination of inspiration and observation is the basis of all human discovery. If you were not inspired as Newton was, you might watch a thousand apples falling from trees without getting any further.

But, Nokes will ask, why do you say that the message that you find in the gospels is different in kind? Why should I not be a stoic or a Hindu or even a scientist—for the pursuit of science, you seem to suggest, is a rather primitive and imperfect religion. It is a fair question, because although I have made many points about that message there is one still to be made that is absolutely central.

2   THE HEART OF THE MESSAGE

In one of Charles Williams's strange novels, there is a girl

whose secret life is dominated by something which fills
her with black panic.[2] She meets her own image;[3] she sees
herself, walking towards her in the street. It *is* herself. It
fills her with indescribable and irrational terror. So far it
has always turned away but one day she is sure that it will
meet her and then she will go mad or die. She never knows
when she will see it and lives in perpetual dread. A poet,
who notices her haunted look, persuades her to tell him
what it is that frightens her. Reluctantly—because it is
something that no one else can possible understand—she
tells him. He asks if he may be allowed to carry her fear for
her. Bearing each other's burdens he goes on, is much
more like carrying a parcel than is commonly supposed.
She will not at first believe that he can help but at last she
says he may carry her parcel and by a powerful effort of will
and imagination he takes her fear on himself and she is
released from her burden and filled with a new joy, simply
in being alive and playing with a kitten.

This is what Charles Williams calls substitution, or
sometimes the doctrine of substituted love, and it is central
to his feeling about Christianity, running right through his
novels and his A *Short History of The Holy Spirit in The Church*.
He also calls it 'exchange' and the result of it he calls 'co-
inherence'. To me the incident is a parable that illustrates
the meaning of Christ's life and death. I have never been
able to stomach the way it is presented by Milton. Man has
sinned and so:

> Die he, or Justice must; unless for him
> Some other able, and as willing, pay
> The rigid satisfaction, death for death ...

This, it seems to me, is Nobodaddy speaking, the voice of
the headmaster who cannot bear to have the rules broken.
Picture instead a loving Purpose—who has given man
freedom and seen him misuse it, who has seen him tearing
himself to pieces, killing his brother, puffing himself up

with self-importance – has seen him, with half the world dying of malnutrition, saying that Charity begins at home; picture that Purpose, sorrowing as you or I would for a son in trouble, making a new offer of partnership, being born as a human child in order to take the manhood into God, offering to carry the parcel of guilt and fear and pain for anyone who would let him, much as the poet offered to carry the parcel for the frightened girl. Then you have an offer of atonement in the sense of making at one; you have a God sharing humanity's pain – born in blood and pain, as other children are, dying in blood and pain, sharing humanity's suffering, yet said by men to be gluttonous and a wine-bibber; firmly rooted in matter, making humanity one with himself.

This is the meaning of that ancient prayer that begins: 'Soul of Christ, sanctify me … ' It is the meaning of the nine-fold invocation at the beginning of the central rite of the Church: 'Lord have mercy upon us … ' We ask in that invocation that the parcel may be carried, that we may be made one with the Eternal Word – and that requires mercy because of our imperfections. It is the prayer uttered by the poor man who stood at the back of the church.

Every birth is a miracle. Every birth is an incarnation of something that may become in some small way divine. A separate human will comes into existence, at first responding only to its animal desires, to the urge to survive and assert itself, conscious of itself as the centre of the world and of the rest of the world only as affecting itself. But gradually, if it is born to loving parents, in the warm enveloping broth of a tradition that does not shut itself off from the Holy Spirit, it may learn to take as its ruling principle artistic creation or healing or a divine concern for others or something of all three. Or it may, since we have freedom, develop into a Hitler or a de Sade.

Every birth, I repeat, is an incarnation of divine possibility. That one birth which bisected time was more. It was the sacramental sign of partnership with man, of the divine purpose carried to its highest pitch. That birth and that death were themselves the heart of the message. It is the essence of John's gospel that men had been in touch with something so holy that it transfigured existence; it is enough, he says, to know that human life has been taken into the divine and everything else follows. The more conscious you become of the Incarnation and all that it implies the more clear will be the law of your own being and the need to fulfil it. And that is freedom.

That birth, that life and death are the heart of the Message, but the teaching of course is part of the life and of the message. The whole message – life, death and teaching – was delivered to a small group of fishermen, cultivators, petty officials. It had to be put in terms they could understand. It had to reach their hearts with immediate impact and be transmitted by them in a form they could remember. One stage of the Incarnation was a weak human child in a mortal body. That made the message human. But that it had to be remembered, that it had to be transmitted through fishermen and recorded by a tax-collector and a doctor, made the message even more completely human. That was a second stage of the Incarnation.

Here we come on another paradox. The Incarnation is something that everyone has to make personally his own and come to terms with in his own way, and at the same time there is a traditional wisdom that is to be disregarded only at grave peril. The Church is in one sense fallible almost by definition; it is human, its leaders have sometimes been corrupt. But again and again, in the great decisions of interpretation which it had to make, the Church was guided by the Holy Spirit. It was right to reject the great heresies I touched on in the Third Interlude, to assert that the creation was good, that man could not be self-sufficient, that the Word had truly been made flesh. But although it is perilous to pick and choose and make up a private little religion of your own, hardly anyone can give equal weight to every aspect of the tradition. For ordinary people who are far indeed from being saints, it is surely legitimate to concentrate on one aspect of the Message. For me it is Christmas and the Incarnation.

But there is still some fight left in Nokes. You have half admitted, he will say, that in the end all religions are the same; the Eternal Wisdom is what men seek and it is One. May it not be reached by other ways?

One Other Way

That there are other ways, I agree unequivocally. Hinduism and Islam are the two other religions of which I have seen most and I have never doubted that a Hindu or a Muslim who seeks the Eternal Wisdom is a better man – that is, he is fulfilling the law of his being more completely – than someone who, though born into the remains of Christendom, does not make that effort. Such a Hindu is coming to the Father by the help of the Incarnate Word though he does not know it. Let me add that it is not fair to remember that there are places where Islam appears still to tolerate slavery without remembering that Christianity, which is six hundred years older, tolerated slavery in one great country until 1864 and serfdom in another until 1861. It is not fair to reproach Hinduism with caste and child marriage and to forget that Christianity must by the same logic be held responsible for the Inquisition, for the horrors of the Industrial Revolution, for gangsterism in Chicago, for gross materialism and the atom bomb. There is little point in comparing Nobodaddyism with the heights of Hindu philosophy or, on the other hand, the beliefs of a Himalayan peasant about the village godling to whom he offers a goat with the revelations made to St Theresa of Avila or with the great intellectual system of Aquinas. We must compare like with like.

But Nokes wants to make up his mind; he wants a religion. And before he makes up his mind, he wants to look at another kind of formulation. Clearly in a book of this length this can only be done in the most superficial way. The literature of Hinduism is enormous and my knowledge of it slight. Nonetheless, I have admired many Hindus and I have formed an impression of the higher reaches of Hinduism, based mainly on the *Bhagavad Gita*. I have no doubt that the *Gita* is an expression of Divine Wisdom and that it has brought to millions of Hindus an understanding of the divine. But the Hindu and the Christian, though both revelations of divine truth, are very different in flavour, in colour. It is as though the same light had shone through different parts of a stained glass window. Let us look at some verses from the *Gita* and then compare them with one Christian book. First, from the *Gita*, from the Tenth Book:[1]

> ... I am the Self, seated in the hearts of all beings; I am the beginning and the life and I am the end of them all.

> Of all creative Powers I am the Creator, of luminaries the Sun; the Whirlwind among the winds and the Moon among planets.
> I am all-devouring Death; I am the origin of all that shall happen; I am Fame, Fortune, Speech, Memory, Intellect, Constancy and Forgiveness.
> I am the Sceptre of Rulers, the Strategy of the conquerors, the Silence of mystery, the Wisdom of the wise.
> I am the Seed of all being ... No creature moving or unmoving can live without Me.

The speaker is Krishna, who is an incarnation of the Divine principle and it is worth noting that some early European visitors to India thought that the name Krishna was a corruption of Christ and the deity worshipped was some kind of imperfect revelation of the Word. Let me contrast with that passage a revelation shown to a simple

unlearned creature—as she called herself, though she was
by no means altogether unlearned— 'living in this mortal
flesh in the year of our Lord one thousand three hundred
and seventy-three, on the thirteenth day of May.' Julian of
Norwich saw Jesus clearly in a series of visions and he
said to her:[2]

'I it am: the might and the goodness of the Fatherhood. I it am: the wisdom and the kindness of Mother-
hood. I it am: the light and the grace that is all blessed
love.'

And on another occasion:

'I it am; I it am that is highest; I it am that thou lovest;
I it am that thou servest; I it am that thou desirest.'

'I it am.' It has been said that all the Hindu Upanishads
are summarized in the single phrase 'Tat tvam asi' which
means 'That art thou' and refers to the unity of the individual human soul with the divine. And of course the
phrase also recalls the I AM of the Old Testament. But
let us continue with Julian. On another occasion:

He shewed a little thing the size of a hazel-nut, which
seemed to lie in the palm of my hand; and it was as
round as any ball. I looked upon it with the eye of my
understanding and thought: 'What may this be?' I was
answered in a general way, thus: 'It is all that is made.'
I wondered how long it could last; for it seemed as
though it might suddenly fade away to nothing, it was
so small. And I was answered in my understanding:
'It lasts and ever shall last; for God loveth it. And even
so hath everything being—by the love of God.'

Later in the *Gita*, in the Eleventh Book, Krishna reveals
himself to his worshipper as he really is:

Crowned with heavenly garlands, clothed in shining robes, anointed with divine unctions, He showed Himself as the Resplendent One, Marvellous, Boundless, Omnipresent.

Could a thousand suns blaze forth together, it would be but a faint reflection of the radiance of the Lord God.

But when Julian of Norwich saw the Lord, he was hanging upon the cross, his body mangled and bleeding; she saw the flesh dried with thirst, the face discoloured and darkened by blood and suffering. At the last moment, his face changed, he looked at her joyfully and said: 'If I could suffer more for thee, I would.'

Let me go back to the *Gita* and quote some verses from Book XII, which is called *The Path of Love*.

Knowledge is superior to blind action, meditation to mere knowledge, renunciation of the fruit of action to meditation, and where there is renunciation peace will follow.

He who is incapable of hatred towards any being, who is kind and compassionate, free from selfishness, without pride, equable in pleasure and in pain and forgiving,

Always contented, self-centred, self-controlled, resolute, with mind and reason dedicated to Me, such a devotee of Mine is My beloved.

He who does not harm the world and whom the world cannot harm, who is not carried away by any impulse of joy, anger or fear, such an one is My beloved.

He who expects nothing, who is pure, watchful, indifferent, unruffled, and who renounces all initiative, such an one is My beloved.

He who is beyond joy and hate, who neither laments nor desires, to whom good and evil fortunes are the same, such an one is My beloved.

He to whom friend and foe are alike, who welcomes equally honour and dishonour, heat and cold, pleasure and pain, who is enamoured of nothing,.

Who is indifferent to praise and censure, who enjoys silence, who is contented with every fate, who has no fixed abode, who is steadfast in mind, and filled with devotion, such an one is My beloved.

What I have quoted is only a part of the *Gita*; the *Gita* is only a part of the enormous collection of beliefs that make up Hinduism. And yet even this tiny sample does give something of the flavour. Julian is not one of the great saints or doctors, but one woman from millions of believers, all seeing what they believe in some subtly different way. I compare Julian with the *Gita*, not as representative champions of their two religions, but simply to illustrate how much there is in common and yet how different is the essence. Compared with Julian, the Beloved of Krishna is altogether impersonal and generalized. Julian is precise about the date of her experience; she was a real person, mentioned in other writings of the time; she is cheerful, personal, earthy. She says on one occasion: 'Glad and merry and sweet is the blissful lovely looking of our Lord into our souls.' And again she says: 'Our courteous Lord willeth that we be as homely with him as heart can think or soul can desire'—but again we must not 'take this homeliness so recklessly as to forsake courtesy'. It is all very human and for some perhaps too simple and earth-bound. But life is earth-bound although we are amphibious.

Julian's book is called *The Revelations of Divine Love*
and the *Gita*, which has been called the Song Celestial, is
also about divine love, or perhaps rather love for the
divine. But they do not mean the same thing by 'love'. The
Hindi word is bhakti, devotion to God, and it is sometimes
translated 'faith' but it is warmer than that, a passionate
love for God. Julian means by 'love' the love of God for
man, of man for God, and of men for other men. But bhakti
is love for God and does not include love for one's fellow-
men. Here too in the *Gita* there is an Affirmative Way and a
Negative Way, but the Negative Way seems to me much
stronger.

Julian saw that God made all and that God loves all.
But for the *Gita* God *is* all. Yet the disciple must reject
desire and the snare of the senses and his aim—like that of
the Manichees—is to *escape* from life and from the cycle of
rebirth. But if all life is God, he is trying to escape from
the God he seeks. Nokes will find here no less paradox than
in the Christian gospel. Again, in the teaching of Jesus
there is always sharp contrast between right and wrong,
even though at first sight the lesson of one parable may
sometimes appear to be contradicted by another. In the
teaching attributed to Krishna, I am left with a feeling that
differences are blurred rather than sharpened—all differences, between right and wrong, between life and death,
between matter and spirit. The framework of the *Gita* is the
dilemma of a warrior on the battle-field who is suddenly
overcome with a feeling that war is futile. Why should he
try to kill men who in some cases are his kinsmen and some
of whom he admires? The reply of Krishna is that he must
perform his allotted function in society. He need not concern himself about these men, whom the Divine Principle
incarnate in Krishna has already doomed to death. The
warrior by whose hand they fall is merely the instrument.
In any case, they will all be reborn.

Surely this reduces the significance of killing and indeed
of most human behaviour almost to nothing. No doubt it is

meant to. That is part of the ache for annihilation, something I do not think I understand. It is a far cry from Christian hope, from the thisness of each created thing, from the message of the Incarnation. It is further still from all that vigorous commitment to practical affairs that is commonly called the Protestant ethic. As for rebirth, behind it lies the social philosophy that each member of society – priest, warrior, peasant or servant – should perform the function to which he has been born and there is no injustice in this because good fortune in this life is the reward for good behaviour in a previous life. It must be consoling for the fortunate to reflect that their happy lot in this life is a re-ward for good behaviour. But for me it is hard to under-stand in what sense it is the *same* soul or spirit that is reborn. It has a different body and since it cannot remember the past, I do not know what identity it shares with the indivi-dual for whose virtue it is rewarded or for whose failure it is punished.

I do not share much physical tissue with the child who was baptized seventy years ago in 1906. Still, the replace-ment has been gradual; at any one moment, something physical was shared with the child or man of the previous few years. Memory, too, though selective, knits me to that child by a series of impressions that no one else can recall. An identity, a character, has been gradually built up, from an immense variety of acts, scenes, influences, conversa-tions. At present that identity is firmly linked to a body in time and space. A Christian must believe that, in some way quite beyond our comprehension, that identity will continue timelessly after death, as a state of separate aware-ness that will perhaps eventually merge in a larger aware-ness – nonsensical though it is to use words implying time, but we cannot rid ourselves of time as a condition of thought. But that identity would have vanished entirely if 'it' – if 'I' – were reborn as a scavenger in punishment for wrongdoings in this life. In what way would it be 'I'? How can it be called the same person? The idea of rebirth has

ONE OTHER WAY165

appealed because it seems, if you do not reflect very deeply, to provide an answer to injustice and inequality, but it would only do that if the new-born scavenger could remember the happiness he had formerly enjoyed as a Brahman. If the soul has any meaning at all it must mean some continuing identity.

I am doubtful whether Nokes will feel, on deeper inquiry, that Hinduism will give him what he seeks. Of course everyone can learn a great deal from another faith. But I am sure that neither here nor in Islam will he find an easy answer. Whether he chooses the spiritual exercises of St Ignatius Loyola or follows some other Christian master whose teaching is less tightly structured, whether he turns to Islamic *sufi* or Hindu *swami*, he will have to concentrate, he will have to work hard, he will need patient self-discipline. He will be told to renounce greed, anger, envy; sloth, avarice and pride. In every system, he will be encouraged to meditate on certain aspects of what he has been taught; he may, in every system, if he perseveres, achieve the height of contemplating eternal truth without 'the determinate words of human discourse'. He will increase his difficulties if he turns to a language, a culture, a habit of thought, quite foreign to his own tradition. Nor will he find any escape from paradox. The search for personal perfection is as hard to reconcile with social duty in a country where people starve to death while the sage sits in meditation, as in one where people grudge one hundredth part of their national income to feed the hungry.

Nokes will have to make up his mind; he will have to choose. By an act of faith, in a spirit of Love, he will have to choose between the unincarnate splendour of the all-embracing All—and the Word made Flesh—manger, maiden's knee, supper with his friends, the spitting, the scourging, the nails.

13

Make Merry with Your Friends

I   NO ESCAPE

As Nokes and I have talked, I have become clear about what I want to say to him personally. I should like him to start on the Affirmative Way, not at first worrying about his shortcomings, but considering the beauty of the world and the achievements of the spirit of man, its courage, its endurance, its suffering, its self-sacrifice. Let him try to think of infinite space and, when his mind is cowed by the silence and vastness of infinity, of a baby too poor to have a cradle; let him try to consider what he means by eternity and come back to all that is involved in eating bread and breathing air. Let him fill his mind with wonder at the thought of birth and death and try to put himself in the presence of the Purpose behind the universe. And then he must consider whether there is not an invisible truth behind visible matter and whether he cannot find what he is looking for in the traditional sacramental faith of Western Europe, whether devotion to the Word made Flesh will not fill that emptiness of the heart.

He will have to find a suitable incarnation for his new spiritual faith.

> But since my soule, whose child love is,
> Takes limmes of flesh, and else could nothing doe,
>   More subtile then the parent is,
> Love must not be, but take a body too ...

He will need in short a Church – in a narrower sense than I

have used the word before – an institution, a community of people with similar beliefs – they will not be identical – and the intention to put them into practice. He will also need to know a great deal more about Christianity than he does; he must make the resolution to channel his vague impulses into some harmony with ancient symbols capable of enormously wide interpretation. He will need to set aside times for practice, for thought and for reading. He will in the course of time become increasingly conscious of his own inadequacy, greed, sloth and folly. But if he accepts the offer made by the Eternal Word to carry that parcel for him, he will begin to feel in a small way at one with that Word; he will begin to feel oned in himself. He has made a loving choice – which he would not have done if he had not been lovingly chosen – and once he has done that he can go so far as the stage he has reached demands, conscious that others are with him and that he is part of a whole.

He will no longer think of a Nobodaddy in scarlet robes and a wig sitting in judgment on miserable wretches who have committed *sins*. He will think instead of the Eternal Word as a touchstone. The existence of the Word is a judgment in itself. Put yourself beside Him and you see how far you fall short. What is judged is a matter of inadequacies and shortcomings rather than breaches of law. Confession is not a trial followed by a sentence but a periodical self-examination and a request for counsel as well as absolution, a discussion of progress or the lack of it and it is likely to be more regular and will be far more valuable if made to a wise priest.[1]

He *may* happily choose a sacramental poverty like St Francis. It is more likely that the Nokes I have come to know will linger for some time in the kind of limbo that St Augustine has drawn so vividly, the long years when he struggled with himself, willing but not willing, praying: 'Lord, make me chaste but not yet!' He will not escape some form of this conflict. But if he says: 'Thy will be done' often enough he may eventually begin to see the truth of that saying, that seems at first sight so hard: 'He who loses his life for my sake shall find it.'

I think he would be wise to take for granted the conclusions of St Augustine in his two great battles with the Manichees and the Pelagians, having nothing to do with the idea that matter is evil nor with the sentimental optimism of supposing that men can forget their animal nature and become perfect by their own efforts. It will help him if he remembers in his rule of life the sacramental principle of regarding certain moments of high intensity as representative and thus enabling himself to take them for granted for most of the time and–again for most of the time–to live with his fellow-men in some degree of comfort, though always, when he stops to think, knowing in his heart that he is a stranger upon earth, and rather an absurd one at that.

As to the four forms of the dilemma which I posed at the beginning, he will have to look on each of them in the spirit I have suggested–on a scale between the sacramental and the idolatrous on the one hand, the Manichaean on the other. It is easy enough to see that some attitudes to money are idolatrous and that some forms of private ownership may be indefensible. What invisible truth does it stand for–the ownership of this piece of land–this share in some commercial enterprise–this house or car? And of poverty, too, the same question may be asked. If poverty is deprivation–not having enough to eat, not having a roof over one's head, not having the means to live in decency–it is an offence that ought to be ended. Sacramental poverty, voluntarily chosen as a vocation, is another matter. Just as certain bread is set aside as a sacrament so are certain men. The truth for which their poverty stands is the unity of all men in common sonship. They take a part of the burden of those whose poverty is deprivation. Their poverty takes its value from the world outside their order for which they work and pray.

The history of the Franciscans shows how impossible

it is to embrace absolute poverty. Today a man has to decide where reasonable provision ends and greed begins and it is seldom a question of giving everything or nothing but of how much to give. In the teaching of the gospels, there is praise for the rich Zacchaeus, who gave half his possessions to the poor, but who still remained rich, as well as for the poor widow who gave the one tiny coin she possessed. But there are two notes that are struck again and again. The first is: do not be *anxious* about money! Do not treat it idolatrously, as though it mattered. And the second is: the right course is to use Mammon to achieve the purposes of God, very much as the Japanese wrestler uses the strength of his adversary in order to throw him. He must behave as a trustee, a steward who never knows when his master is coming.

In respect of force, too, it is almost impossible to present a hard-and-fast yes or no. Even vegetarians, who eschew killing for meat, cannot avoid living in a world in which life is always at the expense of some other life. If they eat grain, the soil is ploughed and a good deal of life destroyed. 'The cut worm forgives the plough'—says Blake—but we have only Blake's word for that. Moles have to be kept out of the vegetable garden; rabbits and squirrels will destroy young fruit-trees and it is not enough merely to drive them into someone else's orchard. The farmer is as much part of the process of life as the hunter; he cannot eat without killing. The lions roaring after their prey do seek their meat from God—yes, but if they do not get it, they may turn their attention to the cattle of the nearest village—or even to the villagers, causing an awkward problem for the non-violent conservationist.

There is a vivid picture in my mind as I write. It was forty years ago but the scene is still clear in memory. A tiger was coming back to the body of a deer he had killed. It was a little before sunset and the monkeys and jungle-fowl were settling for the night. Their startled cries told me a tiger was moving somewhere near. At last I saw him,

huge beneath the trees. I knew that a tiger will kill at least a
hundred deer or cattle in a year; that evening I meant to
kill him. I felt at one with the whole jungle, with the creatures disturbed and frightened by his coming. I felt curiously
a part of nature, almost perhaps as the warrior was meant to
feel when Krishna told him to fight. I was part of a process
much bigger than myself which I could no more understand that I could understand the tiger's destructive force
or his beauty as he came – silently, cautiously, but swiftly –
to the shattered deer, his coat glowing in the evening light,
his eyes burning a clear topaz.

Or watch a fledgling cuckoo hoisting its companions
in a reed-warbler's nest one by one laboriously to the rim
and toppling them over – something I have seen only on
television. There is no room for judging such behaviour
in human terms. Millions upon millions of years have
taught it what to do, just as they have taught it that it must
fly to Africa as soon as it is ready and that to fulfil the law of
its being it must come back to England to shout from every
copse that spring has come. You may call it blind chance; I
see a force, a power, a purpose, beyond my comprehension,
something that can be ruthless, destructive, wasteful, something the Hindus perceived when they put Siva the Des-
troyer beside Vishnu the Preserver. The harvest fields of
evolution are dunged with rotten death, but in the end there
will grow in them the human form divine, 'where Mercy,
Love and Pity dwell'. But the Christian remembers the
Cross as well as the Incarnation; he knows also that:

> Cruelty has a human heart
> And Jealousy a human face;
> Terror the human form divine
> And secrecy the human dress.

We cannot stop the world and get off. We must take
part in the exchange between different levels in the chain of
existence, the continual barter between life and death,

between salts and phosphates, rotting vegetation, new green
life and animal energy – and all we can hope for is a fair
profit on each day's deal. There may be times when it is
right to kill a tiger, a fox, a hijacker or a man with a bomb.
It was right to fight Hitler. What Christianity insists is that
the hijacker and even Hitler must not be hated.

As to sex and the self, here too the message of the Incarnation, the scale between the sacramental and the
Manichaean, between the sacramental and the idolatrous,
provide the touchstone for the individual. But what is a
Christian to do if he lives in a secular, materialist society? I
think it will be clear from all I have said that I utterly reject
the idea that a life of personal piety exonerates a man from
all concern with what is going on in the world. 'Teach me
to care and not to care', says the old prayer; you should do
what you can to put right the wrongs of the world but not
forget how small they are in the face of eternity, nor how
small you are yourself. The message of the Incarnate Word
was for all time but it was left to man to work out its
application to the institutions of each particular age. It
took him a long time to see that slavery was incompatible
with that message. He has to think out what the message
means in relation to the Common Market, to abortion, to
education, to women's rights, to inflation, to whatever the
question of the moment may be. That is his job. That is
freedom. But let him not forget, as he toils in committee
over amendments and points of order, how short is the five
thousand years of history compared with geological time,
nor what a miracle is the emergence of the spirit of man from
the waste solitude of unimaginable light-years.

It would be absurd for one man to attempt to work out,
in terms of the politics and economics of the world we live
in, all the implications of the message. The prisoner has
gone out into the dark alleys of the town and the world is
being fashioned anew. The dangers that face us are obvious
enough. If a remnant should survive an atomic war, their
descendants are likely to be idiots or crippled. If we avoid

that apocalyptic end, we may rot in our own pollution. Never have men been better equipped to survive; we have the technical knowledge to control the population, to feed the world, to dispose of our waste products. What we lack is the organized will, enough people determined to sacrifice some slight immediate advantage in order to prevent total disaster.

Beside the prospect of an end to human beings on earth, beside the contrast of affluence and starvation, the economic crisis in Britain is trivial. Yet the remedy could be expressed in almost the same terms. It is not the means we lack but the will. All we need is a leader who can persuade the whole population to forego some personal advantage for the general good. And I do not mean only national good but the good of the world. There are threats to freedom more serious than the threat to our standards of luxury, not only from tyranny whether of the right or of the left, but from the bureaucratic torpor that already lies upon us 'as sluggish and indomitable as a glacier'.[2]

But if everyone, from the voter upwards, believed that the manhood had been taken up into God, that men had thus become brothers in one fatherhood, our educational system, our public life, our reaction to the hungry half of the world, would be transformed. Does it make sense to be a Christian, I asked at the beginning? Would it destroy society if everyone accepted Christianity? And now I answer emphatically that it does make sense and that nothing else does; that on the contrary, it would save society. But it would be unrealistic in the extreme to expect any such universal conversion.

What I should like to see is a Church that would give form to the formless aspirations of the individual and discipline to his intimations of immortality, that would proclaim its faith with a clear and exultant voice to which the political body as a whole would listen with respect. It is no longer to be supposed that there can be a Church to which all will adhere or a political body that will be unanimous.

But it is possible to picture a society in which there would be agreement on a minimum of ethical principles to which a living church could give assent. If in the future there is to be any political society in which there is freedom, there will certainly be minorities who have formulated their faith in a variety of ways. A living Church which, though widely inclusive, was based on the Incarnation and on a sacramental way of life could give a lead based on respect for the Incarnation and thus for the individual in industrial relations, in education, in medicine, and in much else, to which an allegiance might be won by many who did not subscribe to its doctrine. Even voters will sometimes respond to an appeal to their higher natures.

But the Spirit is at work refashioning the world and I suspect that what in fact is in store for us is as far beyond my comprehension as the thoughts of my mind are beyond the comprehension of one of the millions of cells which, I am told, make up my brain.

2   MAKE MERRY WITH YOUR FRIENDS

As I was coming to the end of writing this book, I heard a discussion on the radio in which a number of women telephoned to the studio to tell of the violence they had endured at the hands of their husbands. Brutal, violent, senseless – if ever there was a sick society it is one in which such things can be common. Only one *man* telephoned; he said he was a reformed wife-beater. He had beaten his wife 'something cruel' four or five times a week for some years. He didn't know why; perhaps because of trouble in his work or not enough money, or just because he couldn't get a cigarette. He wanted to say how he had come to reform. One day he had nearly killed her. He was ashamed and went out. He went into a church. It meant nothing to him but he wanted somewhere to think things out. And the minister had been so kind to him – but here he was stopped. This was a very personal matter, said the chairman of the programme, and what they were discussing was the recommendations of a Select Committee of the House of Commons that there should be centres where such women could take refuge.

Perhaps this is almost as distressing a sign of a sick society as the brutality itself. Turn aside from the evidence of a man who can throw some light on the cause of the disease. It is personal and embarrassing. Keep instead to the steps we must take to deal with the symptoms. That is far less disturbing. But the cause of the embarrassment and the cause of the brutality are one. And it is the cause of murder in Northern Ireland, of vandalism at football matches, of inflation, of bureaucratic torpor. It is emptiness at the heart. Jesus said that if an evil spirit is driven out of a man and that man left empty, the evil spirit will find seven other devils worse than himself and come back. That does not mean that devils should not be cast out. It means that something else should be put in.

I have laid emphasis on beauty, because I think that today it is through a sense of beauty, of poetry, of music rather than through a sense of sin that men will come to take the first steps on the road to a deeper religion. Words are too blunt an instrument; a medley of images is perhaps as far as they can take us:[3]

> The milky way, the bird of Paradise,
> Church-bells beyond the starres heard, the soul's blood,
> The land of spices, something understood.

It is not by chance that the birth of Christ is linked in lovely inconsequence with:

> The rising of the sun
> And the running of the deer,
> The playing of the merry organ,
> Sweet singing in the choir.

But this approach by the path of beauty is not exclusively Christian: it is to be found in Plato. There is Diotima's speech in the Symposium:[4]

> ... he should begin by loving earthly things for the sake of the absolute loveliness, ascending to that, as it were, by degrees or steps ... from fair forms to fair conduct, and from fair conduct to fair principles until from fair principles he finally arrive at the ultimate principle of all and learn what absolute beauty is ...

Yes, but that is a message for the few. Jesus came for the many and forgiveness was at the heart of his message— forgiveness, making at one through forgiveness. There is one parable above all others on forgiveness, a tale short enough, but a gem, not five hundreds words long. Everyone knows it but I want to remind you of it because it is what makes Christian ethics different. 'A certain man had two sons ... ' As so often, I think there may have been a recent event, a story they all knew. The actual father I picture as rather like Count Rostov in *War and Peace*, a kindly loving bumblesome man, careless about his property and not very sensitive about the feelings of his sons. His elder son is narrowly virtuous, strong in a sense of duty, working hard on his father's farm, but always trying to repress a sense of grievance, because no one else works so hard as he does. The younger son—open, emotional, reckless—finds him insufferable. He asks for what in India was called a partition and goes away with a sum in cash that represents his share. The elder son no doubt resented the loss of capital but was secretly glad to be rid of him; the father was grieved and sore, but he would not interfere with the young man's freedom. We all know what happened; the son went away and squandered his capital and had to hire himself out in one of the most despised of jobs. He was hungry and miserable and far from home; he 'came to himself' and was filled with contrition. So he went home and his father ran out and kissed him and would not listen to his penitence but 'put a ring on his finger and shoes on his feet' and ordered a feast. And now the elder son comes in from his work on the farm and finds there is a party—'with music and dancing'— and, when he learns why, he is angry and refuses to go in. His father comes out and begs him to come in but he is still angry; all these years he has worked for his father and never done anything wrong—but his father had never made a party for him, had never even given him a kid to make merry with his friends. And now, he goes on, this son of yours has come back, after wasting your money on harlots, and you do all this for him. Bitter, virtuous, resentful, fully justified—it is easy to hear his tone of voice. And his father gently pleads with him: Everything I have is yours—you have only to ask—but now it is right to make merry because your brother, who was as good as dead to us, is alive; he was lost, he has been found. Oh yes we must make merry!

I suspect that the elder brother had never really wanted to make merry with his friends—but that is by the way. What I want to persuade Nokes is that far too many professing Christians have modelled themselves on the elder brother. But what Christianity is about is the father's reaction to the penitence of the younger son. There is joy in heaven; it is right to make merry.

14

Epilogue: What shall I do?

'But what am I to do?' Nokes asks, turning to me, as I bring my book to an end. 'Almost you have persuaded me. I quite see that it would be unreasonable of me to expect you to tell me what I ought to think about every public issue of the moment. I must make up my own mind about such things. But what am I to do in my own life? How am I to make the start you suggest? And, first of all, what answer am I to give people who say scornfully that religion is at the bottom of half the troubles of the world, that it is because of religion that Protestants and Catholics are killing each other in Northern Ireland and Christians and Muslims in the Lebanon?'

That last question I can answer with some confidence. It is not because of any difference of doctrine that people are killing each other in Ireland. They are not concerned about the relative importance of faith and works or about the Real Presence. They really do not much mind what the other believes. But for three centuries they have been divided into two societies, of different origins, with different customs, each marrying within their own circle, each thinking of the other in generalized terms, not as individual human beings. Religion is the mark by which two tribes have been distinguished, but the distinguishing mark might just as well have been whether they grew beards or practised circumcision or wore bowler hats. They are fighting because one of these tribes acquired the ascendancy and used it ruthlessly to keep the other out of power and jobs and because this deprived group believe they see a chance of reversing the situation. There are of course many other factors involved but none, I suggest, have much to do with religion as I understand it.

But the other question is more difficult. Nokes, you will remember, understands what I am talking about; he is not one of those to whom it is like talking about yellowness to a man blind from birth. He understands the sacrament of the present moment. He has had moments which he remembers in the midst of trivial occupations, moments by which his mind is 'nourished and invisibly repaired'. What he wants is a system that will draw them together, a continuing centre of devotion. He wants a habit of thought that he can count on, just as he counts on the resolution he made long ago that he would get up every morning and not lie all day in bed. He has found already – as I have – that occasional moments are not enough. They are overlaid by the trivial occupations, the cares and riches of the world. I know that I need help, the help that comes from the regular use of sacraments and of set times for self-examination, absolution and counsel. I know how quickly I deteriorate without help of this kind. Nokes, I suspect, is very much like me in this respect. It is no use his just 'going to church'; without some advice he will not understand what is going on and he needs a deeper involvement than occasional attendance at a ceremony which, if looked on in the fashion of the world as entertainment, will be merely boring. It would be very different if he went to church filled with the desire to worship. He needs professional advice; he needs help and also he needs someone to whom he can be of help.

I have to admit that there are frightening dangers. If he were to go to a rigorist who put the letter of the law before personal affection, the Nokes I have come to know would be repelled. It would be just as bad if he fell into the hands of one of those academic theologians who vie with each other in denying the tenets of Christian belief; his hunger would not be fed by any husks of faith they left him. It is sad that such dangers exist, but that is the price of freedom. We must hope that he will find an adviser of simple faith but with a mind sufficiently adventurous to understand the distrust which Nokes and his generation feel for conventions to which they have not given intellectual assent and their passionate concern with human relationships. Such a man will introduce him to people to whom he can himself bring help.

He may find some of those he will meet rather simple, perhaps at first rather dull. They may not be strikingly successful at elegant light-hearted conversation; they may not be 'amusing' in the sense in which people are reckoned amusing at a cocktail party. But if he will remember the words heard by Julian of Norwich – that God made all and that God loves all and that everything has being by the love of God – he will find he comes to look on them in a new spirit, with affectionate laughter for their absurdity – and his own. He will find as a matter of daily experience that the love of God and the love of man nourish each other.

Notes

I have kept the notes to a minimum and made no note where the origin of a quotation is clear from the text. When the notes refer to books in the list which follows, the references are abbreviated.

CHAPTER 2   *The Rich Young Man*

1   See Preface, p. 9.
2   See R. Lloyd, *Letters of Luke* for a suggestion as to how Luke's Gospel may have been compiled. This book is fiction based on thought and study; I had the pleasure of discussing it with the author and find it convincing.
3   T. S. Eliot, *Choruses from The Rock*, vii.
4   Kant, *Prolegomena*.

CHAPTER 3   *First Interlude*

1   The point that different aspects of the same object would be differently expressed was put to me verbally by the late Professor E. N. da C. Andrade, who published it later in his *Approach to Modern Physics*. I discussed it at greater length in *Christianity and Race*. See also his *Mechanism* and *Newton*.
2   John Fowles, *The French Lieutenant's Woman*.

CHAPTER 4   *The Other Cheek*

1   The Moors Murders.
2   I am much indebted to Bhikhu Parekh for his article, 'Fanon's Theory of Violence', which appeared in *Dissent and Disorder*.
3   See *Problems raised by the Use of Force and Violence in the Modern World*: Lecture by Dr Michael Ramsey, then Archbishop of

Canterbury in 1972 and since published in *Canterbury Pilgrim* (S.P.C.K., 1974); also Brookes, *City of God*. See also *Violence in Southern Africa* (S.C.M. Press, 1970).

4 See L. Kuper, *Passive Resistance in South Africa* (Cape, 1956); R. Payne, *The Life and Death of Mahatma Gandhi* (Bodley Head, 1969).

5 Orwell, in an essay on 'Rudyard Kipling' (1942), included in Elliott Gilbert, *Kipling and the Critics* (Peter Owen, 1966).

6 J. McCann, *The Cloud of Unknowing*.

CHAPTER 5 *Second Interlude*

1 See Temple; Barrett; Browning, *A Death in the Desert*. My view of the Fourth Gospel will seem strangely old-fashioned to some modern theologians. That does not make it untrue. John, however, the son of Zebedee, might have been alive in A.D. 100 which is about the time when the Gospel was written. But if I knew that he died twenty or thirty years earlier, it would not affect my belief that the author of this book had been in close touch with someone, probably John the son of Zebedee, who had known Jesus. Certainly, what the author of the Fourth Gospel taught about the meaning of the life of Jesus goes further than had been apparent to the writers of the synoptic gospels, but that is because understanding of the Message was growing. It went on developing and is still developing. I have seen recent articles by professional theologians which appear to discount the Fourth Gospel entirely. Their argument is that Jesus in his lifetime did not claim an *exclusive* revelation and that other religions should not therefore be regarded as outside the divine scheme. But this wider revelation follows from the opening words of the Fourth Gospel itself. If a man believes in a Purpose revealing itself, not by dictation but by guidance, through moments of vision—and surely even a modern theologian must believe at least that—then it is highly illogical to allow the guidance of the Word to Buddha and Mohammad but deny it to the author of the Fourth Gospel. I think this arises from an Arian tendency. Such writers do not believe the Word became flesh. But see chapter 8. 3 of this book.

CHAPTER 6   *Deny Yourself*

1 For the Desert Fathers, see H. Waddell.
2 *Hobbs, Nobbs, Nokes or Stokes.* Robert Browning, 'Popularity'.
3 The passage about Wisdom is not a straight quotation but is put together from Proverbs 8 and Ecclesiasticus 24.
4 Traherne, *Poems, Centuries and Three Thanksgivings*, ed. Anne Ridler (O.U.P., 1966).
5 Donne: use of 'sphere'.

> So thy love may be my loves spheare ...
> *Aire and Angels.*
> Wee are The intelligences, they the spheare ...
> *The Exstasie.*

6 Gerard Manley Hopkins, *Poems*, ed. W. H. Gardner (third edition, O.U.P., 1956); E. Ruggles, *Gerard Manley Hopkins, A Life* (John Lane, The Bodley Head, 1947).

CHAPTER 7   *Hate Your Father and Mother*

1 I understand that recent research goes to show that the nuclear family is older in Europe than was once thought. But I doubt whether this affects my argument. It can hardly be denied that the improvement of communications and increase in mobility since the Industrial Revolution have speeded up fragmentation into the two-generation family and reduced the inter-dependence between kinsfolk living in the same neighbourhood which was once general and still persists in some parts of the country.
2 I am told it is now fashionable to argue that in later life Donne greatly exaggerated his early inconstancy with his 'prophane mistresses', and that the poem I have quoted here ('The Indifferent') was only a tribute to a literary convention. Perhaps. 'Goe and catche a falling starre' and 'Womans constancy' may be conventional but I do not believe it of Elegies XVIII and XIX, nor do I believe that he is there writing about married love.

CHAPTER 8   *Third Interlude*

1 Regarding the mediaeval Manichees I have generally followed Runciman. But see also Knox and Holmes. It is true that a

good deal of what we know about the Albigensians comes either from their enemies or from 'confessions' made under torture or the threat of torture. But Runciman's account is thorough and he traces a convincing sequence of belief from the earliest times to the Albigensian heresy, with some revealing differences. The Inquisition's questionings reveal no traces of 'occult or tantric tradition' among the Albigensians; it does not sound as though the judicial processes were intended to pin on the accused beliefs they did not hold.

2   G. K. Chesterton, *Heretics*. Essay on 'Mr Bernard Shaw'.

3   Nokes may not know that this phrase is to be found in the Athanasian Creed, which in the Anglican church was required by the prayer-book of 1662 to be said in church fourteen times a year, an injunction seldom observed.

4   The assertion occurs in a letter of Arnold Toynbee's quoted in an article by Philip Howard in *The Times*, December 20th 1975. It is sad that so learned a man should take so simplistic a view: his whole argument rests on an Arian assumption and an 'either ... or ... ' concept of the relationship of man to the divine. I am aware that the exact meaning of the term 'Son of Man' is extremely controversial. But here, not for the first time, I have a feeling that theologians have so befuddled themselves with subtleties as to obscure the simplicity that stares them in the face.

CHAPTER 9   *Do This*

1   Quoted in Warnock, *Ethics*; see also Warnock, *Sartre*.

2   The point about habitual recollection and the man sure of his wife's love has been made by Cardinal van Suenens.

3   The present moment: See Augustine, *Confessions*, Bk XI. I speak of the needle on a record-player. Augustine speaks of himself reciting a psalm he knows by heart.

4   I have said more about this in *Kipling; The Glass, The Shadow and The Fire*.

5   Hopkins, 'The Blessed Virgin compared to the Air we Breathe'.

6   The metaphor of the flywheel I have treasured fifty years since I read it in Bosanquet's *Philosophical Theory*.

CHAPTER 10   *Fourth Interlude*

1   Browning, 'Soliloquy of the Spanish Cloister'. See also Sayers, *The Mind of the Maker*.

2   The term 'amphibious' is used by C. E. Osborne *Christian Ideas*.

3   Report in the *Sunday Times*, 21 December 1975 of address by Malcolm Muggeridge at a memorial service for William Hardcastle.

4   St Augustine's conversation with St Monica. St Augustine, *Confessions*, Bk IX. 10. For this well-known passage I have used the translation by R. S. Pine-Coffin in the Penguin Classics except for the last sentence, which is from the translation by Robert Bridges in *The Spirit of Man*.

5   See F. von Hügel, *Philosophy of Religion*, Essay IV, p. 102.

6   T. S. Eliot, *Choruses from The Rock*; see ch. II, note 3.

7   See H. Rahner, *Man at Play*.

8   H. J. Fowler, *Modern English Usage*; Martin Thornton, *English Spirituality*.

CHAPTER 11   *The Heart of the Message*

1   It is strange that anyone should have thought Job patient. 'He will laugh at the trial of the innocent', he says of God and he asks: 'Is it good unto thee that thou shouldest oppress?'

2   Charles Williams, *Descent into Hell*.

3   For meeting one's own image, see Shelley, *Prometheus Unbound* Act 1, l. 191:

> ... Ere Babylon was dust,
> The magus Zoroaster, my dead child,
> Met his own image walking in the garden,
> That apparition, sole of men, he saw.

See also Edgar Allan Poe, *William Wilson*.

CHAPTER 12   *One Other Way*

1   I quote from the translation of the *Gita* by Sri Purohit Swami, a translation dedicated to W. B. Yeats and displaying his influence (Faber, 1935).

2 *The Revelations of Divine Love of Julian of Norwich*; translated by James Walsh, s.j. (1961).

CHAPTER 13 *Make Merry with Your Friends*

1 Confession as a colloquy or discussion of progress rather than a judicial proceeding. See M Thornton, *English Spirituality*.
2 The phrase is Eliot's, in *The Idea of a Christian Society*.
3 George Herbert, *Prayer*.
4 Quoted by Bridges, *Spirit of Man*.

Acknowledgments and Books

Long ago I dedicated *Christianity and Race* to the memory of Neville Gorton, Bishop of Coventry, of whom it was said by Archbishop Fisher that through him blew 'great gusts of the holy spirit'. He introduced me to the Grand Inquisitor and told me to read von Hügel when I was still at school; years later he told me to read Charles Williams. But my debt cannot begin to be put in such terms as that; every time I met him I felt a gust of inspiration. This book I have dedicated to Hugh Newbold, whose gentle counsel and continued selfless existence have for the last twenty years meant more to me than he can guess.

I am very grateful to the Scott Holland Trustees for entrusting me with the lectures and particularly to Professor G. R. Dunstan, Professor V. A. Demant and Father Martin Jarrett-Kerr, C. R. for their advice and encouragement. Father William Wheeldon, C. R. has most kindly helped by advice on the final version. None of these helpers must be supposed to agree with me.

I have found some difficulty in deciding what books to mention. It would make the list intolerably long to include all the indirect influences of the last fifty years. I have put down books referred to in the text, some books which I read specially for this purpose and found useful and a group of old friends which I read again and again.

READING LIST

Abbott, Walter M., s. j., *The Documents of Vatican II* (Geoffrey Chapman, 1966)
Andrade, E. N. da C., *The Mechanism of Nature* (Bell, 1948)
    Sir Isaac Newton (Collins, 1954)

Barrett, C. K., *The Gospel according to St John* (S.P.C.K., 1967)

Blackham, H. J., *Six Existentialist Thinkers* (Routledge & Kegan Paul, 1952)

Bosanquet, Bernard, *The Philosophical Theory of the State* (Macmillan, 1923)

Brookes, Edgar H., *The City of God and the Politics of Crisis* (O.U.P., 1960)

Chariton of Valamo, *The Art of Prayer: an Orthodox Anthology* (Faber, 1966)

Chesterton, Gilbert K., *Heretics* (John Lane, The Bodley Head, 1919)

Demant, V. A., *God, Man and Society* (S.C.M. Press, 1934)
   Christian Polity (Faber, 1936)
   Religion and the Decline of Capitalism (Faber, 1952)

Eliot, T. S., *Selected Essays* (Faber, 1932)
   The Idea of a Christian Society (Faber, 1939)

Evans, Sydney (chairman), *Teaching Christian Ethics* (S.C.M. Press, 1974)

Farrer, Austin, *Love Almighty and Ills Unlimited* (Collins Fontana, 1962)
   Lord I Believe (S.P.C.K., 1962)

Gore, Charles, and others, *Lux Mundi* (John Murray, 1890)

Hick, John, *Evil and the God of Love* (Macmillan, 1966)

Holmes, Edmond, *The Albigensian or Catharist Heresy: A Story and a Study* (Williams & Norgate, 1935)

Hügel, Friedrich von, *The Mystical Element of Religion* (Dent, 1909)
   Essays on the Philosophy of Religion (Dent, 1921)

Huxley, Julian, *Evolution and Ethics* (The Pilot Press, 1947)
   Evolution in Action (Chatto & Windus, 1953)

Joergensen, Johannes, *Saint François d'Assise* (Perrin, Paris, 1924)

Kant, Immanuel, *Fundamental Principles of the Metaphysic of Ethics* (Appleton-Century, New York and London, 1938)

Knox, Ronald A., *Enthusiasm* (Clarendon Press, 1905)

Leech, Kenneth, *Youthquake* (Sheldon Press, 1973)

Lloyd, Roger, *Letters of Luke the Physician* (Allen & Unwin, 1957)

McCann, Justice, o.s.b. (editor), *The Cloud of Unknowing* (Burns & Oates, 1952)

Maritain, Jacques, *Christianity and Democracy* (Geoffrey Bles, 1945)
   L'Homme et L'État (Presses Universitaires de France, 1953)
   The Peasant of the Garonne (Geoffrey Chapman, 1968)

Martin, David, *Tracts Against the Times* (Lutterworth, 1973)

Mason, Philip, et al, *Violence in Southern Africa: The Report of a Working Party* (S.C.M. Press, 1970)

Moore, Basil, *Black Theology: The South African Voice* (C. Hurst, 1973)

Osborne, C. E., *Christian Ideas in Political History* (Murray, 1929)

Parekh, Bhikhu (editor), *Dissent and Disorder: Essays in Social Theory* (World Univerity of Canada, Ottawa, 1971)

Pelican History of the Church, The,
  1 Chadwick, Henry, *The Early Church* (1967)
  2 Southern, R. W., *Western Society and the Church in the Middle Ages* (1970)
  3 Chadwick, Owen, *The Reformation* (1964)
  4 Cragg, Gerald R., *The Church and the Age of Reason 1648–1789* (1960)
  5 Vidler, Alec R., *The Church in an Age of Revolution* (1961)

Pine-Coffin, R. S., trans., *St Augustine: Confessions* (Penguin Classics, 1961)

Rahner, Hugo, s.j., *Man at Play or Did you ever practise Eutrapelia* (Burns & Oates, 1965)

Reardon, Bernard M. G., *Henry Scott Holland: A Selection* (S.P.C.K., 1962)

Runciman, Steven, *The Mediaeval Manichee: A Study of the Christian Dualist Heresy* (C.U.P., 1947)

Sayers, Dorothy L., *The Mind of the Maker* (Methuen, 1941)

Teilhard de Chardin, Pierre, *The Phenomenon of Man* (Collins, 1959)
  Le Milieu Divin (Collins, 1960)
  The Future of Man (Collins, 1964)

Temple, William, *Readings in St. John's Gospel* (Macmillan, 1950)

Thornton, Martin, *English Spirituality* (S.P.C.K., 1963)

Waddell, Helen, *The Desert Fathers* (Constable, 1936)

Warnock, Mary, *The Philosophy of Sartre* (Hutchinson, 1965)
  Ethics Since 1900 (O.U.P., 1960)

Wiley, Margaret, *Creative Sceptics* (Allen & Unwin, 1966)

Williams, Charles, *Descent into Hell* (Faber, 1937)
  He Came Down from Heaven (Heinemann, 1938)
  The Descent of the Dove (Faber, 1939)
  All Hallows (Faber, 1945)
  The Forgiveness of Sins (Geoffrey Bles, undated)

THE SCOTT HOLLAND LECTURES

R. H. Tawney, *Religion and the Rise of Capitalism*, 1922
C. E. Osborne, *Christian Ideas in Political History*, 1925
William Temple, *Christianity and the State*, 1928
A. D. Lindsay, *Christianity and Economics*, 1930
Walter Moberly, *The Ethics of Punishment*, 1933
S. C. Carpenter, *The Bible View of Life*, 1936
Lionel S. Thornton, *Christ and Human Society*, 1943
Maurice B. Reckett, *Maurice to Temple: the Social Movement in the Church of England*, 1946
V. A. Demant, *Religion and the Fall of Capitalism*, 1949
D. M. Mackinnon, *The Humility of God*, 1952
A. R. Vidler, *Social Catholicism in France*, 1960
Michael Ramsey, *Sacred and Secular*, 1964
G. B. Bentley, *The Church, Morality and the Law*, 1966
Monica Wilson, *Religion and the Transformation of Society*, 1969
H. MacAdoo, *The Quiet Revolution: Moral Theology in the Remaking*, 1973